Lesson Plans for Teaching Writing

Lesson Plans for Teaching Writing

Edited by

Chris Jennings Dixon

Foreword by
Kathleen Blake Yancey

National Council of Teachers of English
1111 W. Kenyon Road, Urbana, Illinois 61801-1096

Staff Editor: Bonny Graham

Manuscript Editor: Amy Bauman

Interior Design: Doug Burnett

Cover Design: Jody A. Boles

Cover Photo: ©2007 JupiterImages Corporation

NCTE Stock Number: 08857

It is the policy of NCTE in its journals and other publications to provide a forum for the open discussion of ideas concerning the content and the teaching of English and the language arts. Publicity accorded to any particular point of view does not imply endorsement by the Executive Committee, the Board of Directors, or the membership at large, except in announcements of policy, where such endorsement is clearly specified.

Every effort has been made to provide current URLs and email addresses, but because of the rapidly changing nature of the Web, some sites and addresses may no longer be accessible.

Library of Congress Cataloging-in-Publication Data

Lesson plans for teaching writing / edited by Chris Jennings Dixon.
    p. cm.
   ISBN 978-0-8141-0885-7 ((pbk))
   1. English language—Composition and exercises—Study and teaching (Secondary) 2. Curriculum planning. I. Dixon, Chris Jennings, 1946–
LB1631.L413 2007
808'.0420712—dc22

                                                                2006101690

Contents

Foreword

I remember when I began student teaching. I had only two classes: one an accelerated grade 11 class in American literature; the second a basic grade 9 English class. For what passed for forever, I waited for the time when these classes—even the basic class, whose students were laconically lethargic on a good day and comatose on a bad—would be mine, when I would manage the class and choose the readings and assign the writing and respond to that writing and then plan the lesson I should have planned in the first place. In other words: I ached for that moment when I would be the teacher who would change the world.

Fast forward. I understand teaching much differently now, although, quickly, I have to note: I still want to be the teacher who changes the world. But I understand myself now as a teacher in context: in the context of my department and my school; in the context of my school's relationship with other schools; in the context of what my students have done before entering my class—and what they will do after. I think teachers have often thought in these terms, and in my own work and in terms of students, I have thought of teaching as including in my classroom all three curricula—the delivered curriculum we see in syllabi and assignments; the experienced curriculum students unpack in the process of encountering the delivered; and the lived curriculum that exists before, during and after the time students work with us (Yancey 1998; 2004).

What we see here inside the pages of this book, however, is another way to contextualize teaching, one more collaborative, one more intentionally collective, one designed to support teachers working together. When Chris Jennings and her colleagues designed this project—a project beginning on one North American coast, migrating to another, and populating other sites in between—they talked about it by way of a specific term. They said that they were working on *curricular alignment*. I thought then, as I do now, that alignment was a powerful concept for explaining the relationship between different opportunities for learning and thus for the teachers inhabiting those opportunities to work together. I might explain my reaction to alignment by referring to my own children. When they were in high school, we spent a lot of time talking about high school, about what made high school a particular culture, about what was fun about it and what was trying, and about how college would be different from high school. And about how we wanted it to be different. It didn't make sense, in other words, to make high school into college any more than it would make sense to make middle school into high school. High school is a special place for a special time—and so, too, for middle school and college. At the same time, while we don't want one experience trying to be the other or delivering the other's curriculum (see *Delivering College Composition* [Yancey 2006] for more discussion of this), we do want an alignment, a meeting up of the one site with the other—sort of like the leaves of a table do, flush—so that students don't fall through in transition. That alignment is what makes the table—and an educational system—whole.

And that's what you see here: efforts of that alignment effort, when teachers from different sites worked together in order to afford students successful transitions. In doing so, teachers learned from each other, created new writing assignments and activities, reimagined teaching and learning themselves as a site where students are necessarily in transition.

As this approach makes for good education, it likewise makes for very good reading.

As you will soon see.

Kathleen Blake Yancey
Tallahassee, Florida

Works Cited

Yancey, Kathleen Blake, ed. *Delivering College Composition: The Fifth Canon*. Portsmouth, NH: Boynton/Cook, 2006.

———. *Reflection in the Writing Classroom*. Logan: Utah State UP, 1998.

———. *Teaching Literature as Reflective Practice*. Urbana, IL: National Council of Teachers of English, 2004.

Introduction

Chris Jennings Dixon

L*esson Plans for Teaching Writing* is the result of classroom teachers asking, "Why are high school students unprepared for college courses?" This question arose from a high school English department chairperson's inquiry to a community college instructor about seemingly academically distinguished high school English seniors being placed into developmental college composition courses. That question soon led to collaborative investigation and experimentation in teaching writing among secondary and postsecondary faculties. From 1998 through 2005, middle school, high school, and college teachers gathered in Writing Coalition workshops to explore innovative approaches to teaching writing, returned to their classrooms to develop and implement strategies, convened regularly to discuss their progress, and refined those approaches to improve their students' readiness for college writing. Building upon their wide range of teaching experiences to address student needs, secondary and postsecondary teachers have contributed to this text, a success-proven compilation of instructional activities for the writing classroom.

For this publication, teachers from the Writing Coalition reviewed and selected favorite strategies that have made writing a fun as well as integral part of their curriculum. The Writing Coalition, faculty teams composed of college personnel from ten two- and four-year institutions in partnerships with secondary school teachers in eight states, evolved from an original partnership between Tidewater Community College and Salem High School, both of Virginia Beach, Virginia. Supported by the U.S. Department of Education's Fund for the Improvement of Postsecondary Education (FIPSE), teachers came from the following sites:

> Arizona: Arizona State University—Sam Fees Middle School
>
> California: California State University, Fullerton—Buena Park High School
>
> Florida: Florida Community College, Jacksonville—Wolfson High School
>
> Georgia: Georgia Perimeter College—Towers High School

Michigan: Southwestern Michigan College—Ross Beatty High School

North Carolina: Forsyth Technical Community College— Parkland High School

South Carolina: Greenville Tech College—Woodmont High School

Virginia:

Tidewater Community College—Green Run, Kellam, Landstown, and Salem High Schools

J. Sargeant Reynolds Community College—Lee Davis High School

John Tyler Community College—Lloyd C. Bird High School

At each site, participants collaborated to identify and implement instructional approaches for student success in writing.

Regular communication, national and regional workshops, and site visits by project personnel brought teachers together to share progress and brainstorm strategies. Teams of teachers opened their classrooms for innovation and demonstration, extended classroom practices into writing center methodologies, and created cultures to promote student accountability. For example, some of the high school and college teachers were initially suspicious of the portfolio method. After exposure to this process through workshop and roundtable discussions, these teachers set aside their reservations and experimented with collection, reflection, presentation, and assessment concepts in their classrooms and institutions. (For further discussion of the Writing Coalition Project, refer to Appendix A.)

Before you, we present practical instructional ideas that have worked in our classrooms. Each teaching idea includes the purpose of the activity, necessary preparation, required props and materials, the process and procedure for implementation, instructional pointers and/or possible pitfalls, and ponderings by the teacher to provide "behind-the-scenes" insights into the activity. Additionally, some of the activities demonstrate how teachers use the Internet to enhance interaction in their classes. In planning this text, teachers identified the major areas of instruction in their classrooms as writing process, portfolios, literature, research, grammar, writing on demand, and media. Therefore, this book is divided into those seven sections, with each section organized in sequentially based skill development.

In *Lesson Plans for Teaching Writing,* you will find resources for motivating and engaging your students in writing. These activities have been developed by real teachers in authentic classrooms. However, as one teacher comments, "Teachers are notorious thieves! We borrow ideas from anyone who offers them." Likewise, the following activities have been amended, altered, and elaborated to fit specific student levels and curricular objectives. Feel free to use them as stepping off points to meet your individual instructional needs. As one team member commented on reading a draft of our teaching ideas, "I've got my thumb on something I really want!" It is our hope that you, a teacher like us, will find something to "borrow" from these pages.

I Writing Process

"How do we motivate our students to really care about their writing?" This section contains starting points, revision techniques, and student assessment approaches necessary to guide students in the writing process. To promote student control of individual writing processes, instructional activities have been devised to empower students to find their own voices, make authentic reading and writing connections, and engage in meaningful cooperative learning activities. A concrete demonstration of the writing process may also be found in a high school writing center. Designed for the one-on-one teacher–student interaction that is not always possible in the class period, the writing center promotes student participation in the writing process through active engagement in prewriting, writing, and revision strategies outside of classroom instruction. Teachers who have been exposed to writing center approaches to the writing process find that their roles in their classrooms are altered by their experiences. Instead of instinctively reaching for a red pen to grade a paper, teachers become writing coaches. Additionally, students who engage in reader–writer interactions, whether in the classroom or a writing center, become more reflective about their own writing processes.

LESSON 1
SQUIDS WILL BE SQUIDS! MOTIVATING
IDEAS WITH FABLES

Wendy C. Kelleher

Purpose

- To identify and practice the Six Traits of Writing concept with an emphasis on "ideas"

Preparation

Review the Six Traits of Writing (ideas, voice, word choice, organization, sentence fluency, and conventions) in Vicki Spandel's *Creating Writers through 6-Trait Writing Assessment and Instruction*, 4th ed.

Props/Materials

- *Squids Will Be Squids! Fresh Morals, Beastly Fables* by Jon Scieszka and Lane Smith
- Paper and pencils
- Famous morals written on slips of paper (for those students who can't think of a moral or don't know any annoying people)
- If you're interested in reading more about Jon Scieszka, go to Scholastic's website: http://teacher.scholastic.com/writewit/mff/fractured_fairy.htm

Process/Procedure

(The following is a suggested teacher dialogue with the students.)

1. Attention grabber (anticipatory activity)
Have you ever come across any kinds of bossy, sneaky, funny, annoying, dim-bulb people? Have YOU ever been a bossy, sneaky, funny, annoying, dim-bulb sort of person? Have you ever done anything really silly but then found that it was okay because you learned an important lesson?

Well, long ago, a man named Aesop met a whole bunch of bossy, silly, funny, annoying, dim-bulb people, and he wanted to do something about it. He decided to write stories about these people, and end each story with a lesson we all can learn from bossy, silly, funny, annoying, dim-bulb people. But he didn't want to hurt anyone's feelings, so he changed the names to protect the not-so-innocent. Actually, he didn't just change names, he changed the people . . . into animals! That's what fables *are—stories with animals instead of people as the main characters. Fables also have a lesson at the end called the* moral *of the story. And fables are really short, like a joke . . . usually only one page or so.*

Today, we're going to write some fables—lessons we've learned as we've traveled through life. And we're going to add a moral to the end of our stories. First, though, I'd like to share a few fables written by two famous writers named Jon Scieszka and Lane Smith. These are names you might remember from their other famous books, The Stinky Cheese Man and Other Fairly Stupid Tales!, The True Story of the Three Little Pigs, Math Curse *and* Baloney (Henry P.)

2. Language product (a literary product from the outside world by a famous author)
Just to give you a little background on the whole fable thing . . . this is the introduction for Squids Will Be Squids. (Read the introduction aloud.) *These are examples of fables.* (Read "Grasshopper Logic" and "Frog's New Shoes.")

3. Brainstorming/feedback: Freewriting activity
It's time for us to brainstorm. That means let your brains just go crazy, like a wild storm of ideas, flying this way and that, not even raising your hand, but shouting out your thoughts. I'll record your thoughts on the board as fast as I can.

- *What are the parts of a fable?*
- *What is a* moral*?*
- *Who are the characters in a fable?*
- *How long is a fable?*

4. Directions for writing activity: Directions are detailed about what steps to follow but open to creative innovations.
Now you have an idea of what goes into a moral. Let's talk about how to come up with ideas for our own fables.

- *Choose a moral from those written on these slips of paper OR think about some really "bossy, sneaky, funny, annoying, dim-bulb" people who learned an important lesson.*
- *Then think about a story that illustrates what they did that was silly ("Frog's New Shoes" or "Grasshopper Logic").*
- *Next, think about the lesson they learned: That's the moral of the story.*

- *Last, make these people into silly animals representing people. There's your fable! Just get all your thoughts on the page and then we'll rearrange them into an interesting fable.*

5. Share a teacher-written sample of the activity.
While you're thinking about bossy, sneaky, funny, annoying, dim-bulb people to write about, I'm going to share the fable I wrote about a silly thing someone did once and the lesson they learned ... to give you more ideas about what you can write.

6. Students begin writing. (Use paper and pencil, not computer yet.)
Okay? Does everyone know what we're doing? Ready, set, WRITE—fable time. We'll share our fables at the end of the class period.

7. Individual attention: At the end of the writing period, read the "Very Serious Historical Afterward."

Pointers or Pitfalls

Gently encourage any students who say they can't think of anything to write. Ask them about their favorite fairy tale and "bend" it a little for humor's sake.

Ponderings

Students seem to love bending fairy tales and writing about annoying people. This is especially true with teenagers, who get easily annoyed. Encourage the students to be kind to each other, though. This activity could offer the students a chance to pick on someone in the class or be cruel in some way. Watch out for that.

LESSON 2
TRAVEL DIARY: FROM PREWRITING TO PRODUCT

James Blasingame Jr.

Purpose

- To provide prewriting experience
- To make reading and writing connections

- To improve process ideas, word choice, and sentence fluency in writing

Preparation

Collect as many different travel brochures as possible to as many exotic locations as possible. The goal is to have enough material so that
the students have some degree of choice of location. Choosing one of
the brochures, the teacher writes her or his own travel diary alluding
to the items in the brochure.

Props/Materials

Enough travel brochures to exotic places to give students a selection of
choices of location for this writing activity.

Process/Procedure

The teacher opens class by asking students about the best and worst
vacations to distant places they have experienced and then uses color
transparencies of a few travel brochures to illustrate what the typical
brochure looks like. The teacher has already written a one-week fictional
travel diary that matches one of the brochures and shares this travel
diary with the students, again showing the brochure panels relevant to
the diary. For example, the brochure may have a picture of beautiful
tropical fish swimming with scuba divers on a colorful reef, and the
diary describes a day of scuba diving that may or may not be as the
brochure depicted it. Some humor might be appropriate here.

Student travel diaries become part of a wall display with diaries arranged beside the brochures they used.

Pointers or Pitfalls

Since Travelocity.com and other Internet sources seem to be making
travel agencies a thing of the past, it may be necessary to print travel
ads off the Internet, which is fine and may give the teacher more options. Some travel ads may include inappropriate activities for minors,
such as drinking and gambling, so be proactive in saying the travel diary may not include activities that are considered illegal or immoral.

Ponderings

It is wise to think of the likelihood that students in the school may not
be familiar with the concept of travel to an exotic vacation location, so

use the set up time to prime them accordingly. Just because students have done little traveling outside of their area is no reason to avoid this activity; it just requires a little consideration and explanation that this is an activity of the imagination. Although students may not have traveled extensively, they have seen much of the world on television.

LESSON 3
THE ALIEN: USING SPECIFIC DETAILS

Mary Kay Crouch

Purpose

- To understand the notion of audience and practice using specific details

Preparation

This activity creates a scenario for writers to imagine who the reader might be and what she or he needs to fully comprehend the message and for readers to recognize the importance of a writer's use of specific details in effective communication.

No special preparation is needed for this assignment although butcher paper may be useful.

Props/Materials

The Alien handout (Figure 1.1), paper, and a pen or pencil. (Keep it simple, especially the drawing, although you may want to allow students who do a good job of providing details to produce more colorful drawings, if they're so inclined.)

Process/Procedure

1. All students draw their idea of what an alien might look like.

2. Next, each student writes directions for creating the alien she or he has drawn.

3. Then students exchange *only* the directions. You may want to redistribute these or simply have students exchange them with a neighbor.

4. The second student follows the written directions for drawing the alien and attempts to reproduce the drawing. Students are not to talk to one another during this drawing phase. The idea is to use only the written directions to create the other student's alien.

5. Finally, when the second drawings have been completed, students compare the drawings they have made, using the written directions, with the original drawings. You should show the class those who got closest to the drawing by following the directions. Let everyone see the drawings side by side. Look at those directions and discuss why they are so effective.

Pointers or Pitfalls

Students may be hesitant to draw because they worry what they produce won't be artistic enough. Assure them that this has nothing to do with art. It is sometimes difficult to get the students to focus on the purpose of this assignment rather than on the drawings. Keep bringing them back to the idea that we write for a reader. Have them think about how clear their directions are for readers trying to recreate the alien from them.

Ponderings

One technique to keep students on track with this assignment is to ask them to reflect in a brief journal about the success (or not) of their directions. They might also answer these questions: What made the successful directions successful? Depending on the class, how might they use what they've learned to write more successfully? Why is audience consideration so important?

The Alien

1. Preparation
Please take out a sheet of paper and draw your version of what you think an alien from outer space would look like. This doesn't require any artistic talent. Do the best you can.

Now, on another sheet of paper, write directions for drawing the alien you have created.

You will exchange the written description of the alien with another student, but please keep your drawing with you. (And don't show it to anyone.)

2. Activity after the exchange
You now have written directions for drawing an alien someone else has created. Please draw this alien, but don't ask for the creator's help or for help from any other students.

3. Follow-up
When you finish your drawing, take it to the student who created it and ask to see the original she or he created.

Consider these questions and discuss them with others:

- For the reader/draw-er: You were a "reader" and a "draw-er" for this activity. What kind of information would have helped you do a better job with the drawing you had to make?

- For the creator of the alien: Looking back on the directions you made for the "reader/draw-er" of your alien, as you created your directions, what do you now think you might have done better to make your directions easier to follow? In other words, what kind of information do you think your reader needs from you as a writer?

Lesson Plans for Teaching Writing edited by Chris Jennings Dixon © 2007 National Council of Teachers of English.

Figure 1.1

LESSON 4
DOUBLE DOUBLE STORIES: IMPROVING WORD CHOICE

Melissa Reid

Purpose

- To improve word choice and sentence fluency

Preparation

Tell the students that you are going to read them a story that has wonderful word choice. The words may come out as nonsense words, but they will still make sense to the students. Tell students to pay attention to all of the "double" words that they hear in the story.

Props/Materials

Copy of *Double Trouble in Walla Walla* by Andrew Clements, butcher paper in big sheets, boxed markers.

Process/Procedure

1. Read the picture storybook *Double Trouble in Walla Walla* to the students. Be sure to point out the illustrations by Salvatore Murdocca as well.

2. After reading the story, have the students get into groups of four to five students. Give each group a box of markers and two sheets of butcher paper. On the first piece of paper, the group needs to come up with as many of the double words that they can remember from the story.

3. After about five minutes, ask each group member to circle their favorite TWO double words that are on their paper. (There will be eight to ten words circled when they are finished.)

4. On the other piece of paper, assign students to write a story with their group using all of the double words that they circled.

   Note: To help with the paragraph assignment, give each group a small piece of paper with the title that they need to use for their paragraph. Examples of titles are "The Bike Accident," "The Dance," "Dinner at Uncle Ed's House," or "Grounded!" After giving the groups time to write, ask students to share their work with the class.

Pointers or Pitfalls

Be sure to read the story aloud a few times on your own to make sure that you don't get tongue-tied. It's a fun read-aloud, but it can get tricky if you don't practice beforehand.

LESSON 5
BEING THERE: USING SPECIFIC DETAIL IN NARRATION

Marty Brooks

Purpose

- To develop awareness of the different ways specific details make narrative writing engaging and effective

Preparation

This exercise should follow a discussion of the purpose of narrative writing (either personal, nonfiction, or fiction), emphasizing the fact that narrative writing often attempts to make readers feel as if they are experiencing an event through selected images, events, and perspectives. Choose a narrative text and a paragraph in that narrative text that effectively uses specific detail. I have used many different articles for this. However, the example that I will use for these directions is an excerpt found in *The St. Martin's Guide to Writing*, 6th ed., Annie Dillard's "Handed My Own Life" (*The St. Martin's Guide to Writing*, 6th ed., 29–30). Ask students to read the essay before this exercise (either in class or as homework).

Props/Materials

A narrative text (either from a textbook or photocopied).

Process/Procedure

1. After a general discussion of the purpose of the narrative text that the students have read, focus on one scene in that text that uses specific detail effectively. For instance, I often use the following paragraph:

> Father had stretched out his long legs and was tilting back in his chair. Mother sat with her knees crossed, in blue slacks, smoking a Chesterfield. The dessert dishes were still on the table. My sisters were nowhere in evidence. It was a warm evening; the big dining-room windows gave onto blooming rhododendrons. (Dillard 30)

2. Discuss what the specific details say about the characters and situation and note that the passage includes characters' broad actions, mannerisms, dress, and their surroundings.

3. Next, ask the students to use the techniques that they discovered in this passage to do the following:

> Write a detailed description of two people eating together. From this description, the reader should get a sense of who the people are, their relationship to each other, circumstances under which they are eating. Use so many specific details that you start feeling absurd. (You might mention brands, types of clothing, smells, mannerisms, hairstyles— go all out.) You can create any scenario. You can imagine and describe your grandparents in their kitchen, two homeless people eating in the park, two friends at a ballgame, etc.

Give the students at least thirty minutes to write. As they work, prod them to go into greater and greater detail.

4. Finally, choose four or five students to read their scenes aloud to the class.

Pointers or Pitfalls

Often students are embarrassed to read aloud. You may offer to read the student work yourself. Also, you need to make this a fun activity. Encourage students to get as detailed in their narratives as possible and, as they do, look over students' shoulders. Humorously push them to eliminate vague descriptions by asking questions: What kind of "bad" do you mean? Is she twelve young or twenty young? What kind of chicken is she eating? Students enjoy the extremely different scenes that they create from this exercise and they are surprised at how effective their narrative writing sounds. Note that the scenes that they create should mirror and expand on the model that they are presented. If you give them a paragraph or scene that describes a snowball fight, have them write their own description of a snowball fight. If the example describes a wedding, have them write their own description of a wedding.

Ponderings

This exercise is particularly helpful for those students who say that they have no idea how they can write three pages on an event. It graphically demonstrates that they are able to use description and expand on and present a scene in detail. It also shows them that such detail is not just adding words to meet a page length, but that specific detail can help make narrative writing engaging, rich, and effective.

LESSON 6
"I'M SORRY" LANTERNS: USING DESCRIPTIVE LANGUAGE

Melissa Revel

Purpose

- To use language descriptively and creatively

Preparation

Provide a model of a previous prepared lantern for students to see as an example.

Props/Materials

Paper, colored paper, crepe paper, glue, hole punch, string or yarn, and markers.

Process/Procedure

1. On paper, students brainstorm times that they were sorry for doing something they probably shouldn't have done. It can be something serious or something funny; it doesn't matter.

2. Next, students use descriptive language to describe what they did to get into trouble and why they are sorry for what they did.

3. Students write about being sorry for the act using words other than *sorry*. They should also be creative with their titles.

4. Students share their work with their peers in editing sessions and revise accordingly.

5. After each student has another student edit the work, students write their final drafts on colored paper.

6. Students align their writing in the middle of the paper because they will roll the paper to form lanterns, then glue the seams closed.

7. Students cut four equal length strips of crepe paper to glue to the bottom, inside each lantern.

8. The teacher hole punches three equal distance holes across the top of each lantern and assists the students in running string or yarn through each hole to make three loops.

9. The students display their lanterns in the classroom as a final product.

Pointers or Pitfalls

Teachers should hole punch and string the lanterns to save time.

Ponderings

These lanterns look great hanging across the classroom, and students enjoy the hands-on experience. It's a fun project!

LESSON 7
PERSONAL INTERVIEWS: WRITING A DESCRIPTION

Mary Virginia Allen

Purpose

- To write a description of another student based on visual observations
- To practice interview skills to gather information about another student
- To write a description of another student using the interview information

Preparation

Discuss the concept of descriptive writing as well as the interview process before doing this activity. Guide students in a whole-class brainstorming activity to develop a set of interview questions. These questions can be written on the board and copied by the students or typed and duplicated by the teacher for the next day.

Props/Materials

No special materials are needed as long as students are prepared with paper and pen.

Process/Procedure

1. The teacher assigns student pairs.
2. Each student writes down as many physical characteristics as possible about his or her partner: eye color, hair, height, freckles, braces, eyeglasses, type of clothing, anything that might be included in a *picture* of that person.
3. Next, each student asks the class-generated interview questions and gathers information about the partner.
4. Students should take careful notes.
5. Finally, each student writes a four-paragraph descriptive essay about his or her partner. This should include an introduction, one body paragraph that describes physical qualities, one paragraph that describes the other stu-

dent according to information gathered in the interview, and a conclusion.

Note: This assignment can be carried over into the next class meeting time for pairs of students to peer edit before individually preparing final drafts for teacher evaluation.

Pointers or Pitfalls

The teacher needs to be wary of placing weak writers with other weak writers. Often, if one writer is more adept, he or she can assist the weaker student to improve his or her writing. However, the teacher should also encourage the stronger writer not to "take over" someone else's work.

Ponderings

If the teacher pairs students of different ethnic backgrounds, this activity has the capability of bonding a diverse classroom of students.

LESSON 8
MUSICAL CHAIRS: PRACTICING TRANSITIONS

Bonnie Startt

Purpose

- To practice use of transitions in organization of writing

Preparation

Assign a writing topic/prompt that is a fun topic that motivates students to follow different paths. For example, think of *Peanuts'* Snoopy's favorite story opener, "It was a dark and stormy night. . . ."

Props/Materials

A sheet of paper and a pen, although this activity can be done in a computer lab.

Process/Procedure

1. Each student begins writing an opening paragraph from the prompt. Allow a reasonable amount of time. Play background music. Classical music can be soothing and conducive to thought.

2. The teacher asks students to stop writing and to walk around the room as the music plays.

3. Students stop moving when the music stops and sit down at the nearby desks where other students' works are waiting.

4. The teacher starts the music again and instructs students to write the words: "Out of nowhere appeared a . . ."

5. The teacher cautions students to include transitions from the first writer's contribution to theirs so that the writing flows smoothly.

6. After a few minutes, the teacher asks students to stop writing and to begin walking again as the music begins.

7. The teacher repeats the process of stopping the music with students sitting at new desks, reviewing the works of past writers, and writing additional paragraphs.

8. The teacher continues the process as long as time allows. It is important to provide ample time for students to write a closing paragraph assignment.

9. Students return to their own papers to write their conclusions.

Pointers or Pitfalls

Allow adequate time for writing and, if possible, plan extra time for a final editing session. It helps to tell the students in advance how much time they have for each section so they can plan their time accordingly.

Ponderings

The chance to share the completed stories is a highlight of the activity. When time is limited, I have placed students into groups and encouraged them to select the papers they like best; the winning papers are then read aloud.

LESSON 9
SOLE STORIES: DEVELOPING ORGANIZATIONAL SKILLS

Mary F. Rezac

Purpose

- To improve ideas and organization in writing

Preparation

Throughout the year, my students write in their journals about various things we do in class, books we read, current events, notes on areas of study, funny things that occur, and reflections on their goals and progress. This activity stimulates students during the first week of school to use the reflective process.

Props/Materials

Student's shoes, drawing paper, student journal.

Process/Procedure

1. During the first week of school, when students are still trying to discover what the class is going to require of them, ask students to take off one of their shoes and set it on their desk. Their first task is to make a sketch of it on paper, drawing it to scale with as much accuracy and detail as possible.

2. Instruct students to turn these drawings in to the teacher.

3. Store the drawings for an end-of-the-year activity.

4 Throughout the year, assign students to write reflections on class work and their progress in journals.

5. Toward the end of the year, return the shoe drawings to the students.

6. Ask students to write a "Sole Story" in their journals from the unique point of view of their shoes. This story is an opportunity for students to "look back" at their year and what they have accomplished.

7. Guide students to write a brief timeline of the events they have chosen to include in their story before writing the draft.

Pointers or Pitfalls

The students love to remember both the best and the worst times of their year. The timeline helps students organize their ideas. I also encourage them to work on a great beginning sentence, for example, "Boy, Kevin really made me work this year, running from one class to the next on the opposite side of campus!"

Ponderings

Class discussion and remembrances can jump-start someone's writing when he or she is stuck. (I try to take lots of pictures throughout the year.) I also remind students that each one of them leaves their "footprints" on everyone they come in contact with each year.

LESSON 10
THREE IN ONE: ANALYZING THINKING PROCESSES

Charles S. Pierce Jr.

Purpose

- To reflect upon individual thinking processes
- To write from a perspective of past, present and future goals in education

Preparation

Talk informally with the class about the project before actually giving the students writing assignments. Discuss your own goals using sample educational experiences. (For instance, students are amused to know that I was really weak at math. I always tell them to check my math on any assignments with a point system and to make sure I average their grades correctly at the end of the semester!) These papers seem to be very useful since they provide a catalyst for students and teachers to share some of their experiences and ideas about education. The sequence also enables the students to move from more informal first person papers (Paper 1 and Paper 2) to a third-person formal paper (Paper 3).

Props/Materials

It is useful to have sample papers for each of the three assignments. If no samples are available, enlist enthusiastic students to hand in rough drafts for class discussion well in advance of the paper due date. (Tell students who help out by providing early samples for discussion that they will get bonus points!) For Paper 3, a good article on American education is necessary. An Internet search by the teacher or student can provide several samples, such as "Urban High Schools Stress Value of College Education" by Laura Pappano (*The Boston Globe*, Nov. 30, 2003, at www.Boston.com).

Process/Procedure

This three-paper project is used best at the beginning of the semester, although I have used it at various points in the semester. It is designed so that students write papers of various degrees of complexity in sequence. Although I have assigned these papers as a group, it is possible to spread them out over the entire semester with other kinds of assignments in between. If students have trouble selecting a topic or want to make sure the topic fits the assignment, they can check with the teacher. Length of paper should be about five hundred words, but papers can be a little shorter or a little longer.

Paper 1

Write a paper about some incident that happened to you during your K–12 school years. For example, a heartbreaker game that you lost at the last minute, a field trip, a quarrel with a classmate, an encounter with a teacher you liked or didn't like. (To keep your readers' interest, be as fair and impartial as possible in explaining an uncomfortable encounter with a classmate or teacher.) If you want, you may make this paper humorous, but be specific and detailed to keep the reader interested.

Paper 2

Write an introspective paper about yourself as a student. (You may use "I", etc.) What do you think your strong areas and your weak areas are as a student? Explain and show how this came to be the case. (If you like, you may focus on one subject that is your best or weakest.) Another way of approaching this topic is to write on what are often called study skills. What are your strong study skills, and what are your weaknesses? How do you go about studying, and how could you improve?

Go into detail and be brutally honest or you won't gain much from this activity.

Paper 3

Please avoid the word *I* in this essay and write in what is called the third person ("students should," "a college education should," etc.). Think about what a college education should involve before you start jotting down ideas for this essay. Also, please read the article that I have assigned.

Write about one or more of the following. You may want to synthesize (combine) some of these questions:

1. Why should a college education be qualitatively, not just quantitatively, different from high school?

2. Why is it important that colleges invite students to think about why they think the way they do?

3. How can a college education help people think more clearly when forming opinions?

4. What should a college student know by the time he or she graduates from a four-year college?

5. Why is it important for college students to keep learning and examining their opinions and learning processes throughout their lives? (Other approaches to what college should help students achieve in terms of learning may be acceptable, but check with me!)

Pointers or Pitfalls

Because each of these assignments requires more analysis than the last, it is not surprising that the narrative papers for Paper 1 may often be the best papers of the three. These papers are usually fresh and amusing. Paper 3 is clearly the most difficult. It is perhaps a leap for students to think about what a college education means—particularly for those who are simply surviving from day to day and have no goals other than getting through the semester after a hard day of flipping hamburgers. Nevertheless, I think an overall introspective paper about what a college education means can wake up some students. Even if students may not do as well on Paper 3, some of the questions related to what thinking means may cause a jump in maturity level later on. Metacognition is certainly not easy for any of us!

Ponderings

For the third essay, I assign a reading on education. I have not found an essay yet with which I am 100 percent happy. An alternative might be to have students find an article of their own about American students and the thinking process or about weaknesses and strengths in American college education to serve as a prompt for this activity. (Check to see if the article will really get students to think about thinking and remind students to document anything they "borrow" from whatever essay is used.) An alternative might be to combine the third essay with a unit on logic so that students can see that we all make mistakes in our logic, and college can help us sort out some of our illogical mistakes. A certain amount of overlap exists among the three topics, so if students become a little confused, that is okay. However, papers such as "my pet pony" are clearly off the topic, and these essays should be sent to "swim with the fishes." In general, students should be encouraged to show the instructor and each other rough drafts or beginnings of rough drafts, to ascertain if the student is clearly focused on an assigned topic.

LESSON 11
"I HATE GROUP WORK": TRANSFORMING CONFLICT INTO COOPERATION

Chris Jennings Dixon

Purpose

- To promote interpersonal skills
- To encourage positive patterns of communication in group work
- To develop dialogue for collective understanding
- To develop conflict resolution techniques for cooperative learning activities

Preparation

Encourage students to engage in collaborative activities that promote appropriate interpersonal communication. These might include, for example, a peer review or a discussion about group work and productive and unproductive conflict. As a motivational activity, ask the students to individually draw their own version of something out of the ordinary, such as "A fish wearing a hat smoking a cigar." Students then share their drawings and discuss their individualistic approaches. Make sure students recognize that there is no one "correct" interpretation. Then lead the students into a discussion of conflict.

Props/Materials

- What Conflict Means to Me handout (Figure 1.2)
- "The 8 Essential Steps to Conflict Resolution" by Dudley Week (1994) available at http://www.thinkingpeace. com/Lib/lib003.html
- Access to conflict resolutions websites:
  - http://www.selectpro.net/index.php/ScrInfoIBA. html?sid=WrTtJgciJIDuwhtK
  - http://disputeresolution.ohio.gov/schools/content pages/styles.htm
  - http://www.qvcc.commnet.edu/classes/ssci121/ Index.htm
- Warm-up Activities for Group Work handout (Figure 1.3)
- Responsibilities for Group Members handout (Figure 1.4)
- Conflict Resolution Techniques handout (Figure 1.5)

Process/Procedure

1. Students complete What Conflict Means to Me handout and share their findings.
2. Teacher guides students in use of website materials to identify their approaches to conflict and resolutions.
3. Teacher guides the class in use of the interpretative materials for students to study the results and reviews suggestions for their conflict management approaches.
4. Teacher uses items from the Warm-up Activities handout with students to enable them to practice skills needed for positive group interaction.
5. Teacher distributes and discusses Responsibilities of Group Members and Conflict Resolution Techniques handouts with students.

6. Teacher assigns students to work in groups for a collaborative project.

Pointers or Pitfalls

Students need to be prepared to work as a group. One common obstacle
to collaboration is that students have learned in school that individual
work is valued, so their idea of learning may include an underlying
assumption of competition with other students. It may be difficult for
some students to let go of that competitive attitude and learn to think
as members of a team.

Students often have issues with grading fairness when assigned
to group work. A student may feel it is unfair to give one grade to the
group rather than individual grades. Adopting a policy that assigns
points for individual student contributions may be used as well as including both self- and peer/group evaluations.

Students need to recognize that conflict is unavoidable in group
dynamics. However, they also need to discover that conflict can produce meaningful results when they approach it in a proactive mode.

Ponderings

Small group work provides an opportunity for students to work together and to maximize their own and each other's learning. Working
in groups forces students to think and does not allow them to be passive learners. Encouraging students to work with others in pairs or
groups is important to establishing lifelong skills. Assisting students in
development of cooperative learning skills, collective understanding,
and recognition of conflict and resolution techniques can help them to
work collaboratively without getting frustrated and discouraged.

What Conflict Means to Me

Think of what *conflict* means to you. Is it scary or exciting? Is it interesting or yucky? Write in the circles words that come into your mind when you think of *conflict*. (Make additional circles if you need to.)

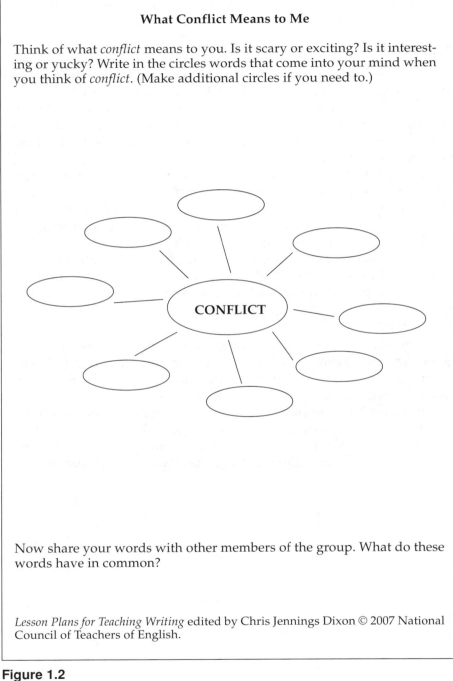

Now share your words with other members of the group. What do these words have in common?

Lesson Plans for Teaching Writing edited by Chris Jennings Dixon © 2007 National Council of Teachers of English.

Figure 1.2

Warm-Up Activities for Group Work

Use the following activities to build interpersonal relationships and promote cooperative approaches.

1. The Magic Wand: You have found a magic wand that allows you to change three school-related activities. You can change anything you want. How would you change yourself, you classroom, your schedule, your sports team? Why would you make the change?

2. Teacher of the Month: You have been selected "Teacher of the Month." What will you change about your class, your school, your community?

3. Survival: You are marooned on an island with five items. What are the five items you have carefully brought with you to ensure your survival?

4. M&M's: Distribute a bag of M&M's, telling students to take as many as they want. Warn them not to eat them YET! Once all the candy has been distributed, each student has to say one thing about himself or herself for each M&M received.

5. Common Strands: Pair the students. Each pair has thirty seconds to find five things they have in common. At the end of the thirty seconds, put two pairs of students together and give the foursome sixty seconds to find something all four have in common. Finally, each group shares a list of the things they have in common with the class.

6. Mathematics Mayhem: Decipher mathematical equations to find hidden messages. Ask students to work individually and then in groups.

    - $36 = I.$ in a Y.
    - $6 = W.$ of H. the E.
    - $212 = D$ at which W.B.
    - $3 = P.$ for a F.G. in F.
    - $20 = Y.$ that R.V.W.S.

    f. $101 = D.$
    g. $60 = S.$ in a M.
    h. $7 = H.$ of R.
    i. $56 = S.$ of D. of I.
    j. $5 = F.$ on the H.

7. Wordles: Decipher verbal symbolic interpretations to find hidden messages. Ask students to work individually, then in groups.

    - SIDE SIDE
    - NOON LAZY
    - IECEXCEPT
    - ONCE
      TIME

    - YOU/JUST/ME
    - DEAL
    - STOMACH
    - NAFISH
      NAFISH

• F		F
R		R
I	Standing	I
E	Miss	E
N		N
D		D
S		S

Lesson Plans for Teaching Writing edited by Chris Jennings Dixon © 2007 National Council of Teachers of English.

Figure 1.3

Responsibilities of Group Members

To develop a team approach to the task at hand, follow these simple guidelines:

1. Be committed to your group goal. Speak up. No one can know your thoughts and feelings. It is your responsibility to communicate what you are thinking. Use initiating comments to start the group process, such as "This looks like an interesting project. Let's begin."

2. Identify your goal and the tasks. Set clear deadlines and schedule frequent meetings. Consider what hurdles may impact the progress of your group.

3. Avoid personal conflicts. If there is a problem, focus on the issue, not the person. Use "I" language rather than "You" language." "You" language tends to place others on the defensive. For example, "I am not sure I understand what you are saying" versus "You are confusing me."

4. Help your group work in a cooperative manner. Make suggestions that bring diverse ideas together, such as "That's helpful information, Rachel. How could you combine it with Jerry's suggestion?"

5. Complete individual assignments. If you say you are going to do something, do it! Agree to be a team player, meet deadlines, and know the rest of your group is counting on you. Be honest in your self-assessment.

6. Encourage everyone in your group to participate. If you notice that someone is not participating, ask him or her, "What do you think?" or "How do you feel about our work so far?"

7. Be sure to listen to each member of the team. Use the following prompts to ensure you are receiving messages sent: "While listening to my partner, I heard . . ." "While listening to my partner, I realized . . ." and "While listening to my partner, I learned . . ."

8. Stay on task. Talking about what happened last night on television or before school may have some relevance to the task at hand and can actually be helpful in creating common ground but be sure to come back quickly to the group goals. Remind your group that you have a purpose to accomplish.

9. At the end of the project, you may be required to complete a self-evaluation for your contributions. Be ready to assess your discussion and group process skills.

10. Fill out peer evaluations of group work honestly and sincerely. Be prepared to express positive and negative experiences of the group experience. A suggested title may be used to reflect your ideas about working on a team, such as "One Thing I Like," "One Thing I Dislike," and "One Thing I'd Like the Team to Have/Get/Do."

Lesson Plans for Teaching Writing edited by Chris Jennings Dixon © 2007 National Council of Teachers of English.

Figure 1.4

Conflict Resolution Techniques

Sample scenario: Steve is working with three other students on a team project. At first, everyone has a different idea about the choice of topics for the team to select. A lengthy debate ensures. Eventually, three of the students agree on one choice; however, Steve does not like their selection and raises his voice about it, disturbing others in the classroom. He makes the other students in his group feel threatened by their choice.

How can this conflict be resolved?

Use the following procedures to resolve conflict:

1. Explain the situation as you see it. Emphasize that you are presenting your perception of the problem. Use specific facts and feelings.

2. Describe how the conflict is affecting the group's performance. Keep your attention on the task at hand and away from personalities involved. Present the problem in a way that is readily understood and concentrate on important issues.

3. Ask for an explanation of the other person's viewpoint. Before proposing a solution, gather as much information as possible. Respect the other's opinion and request his or her cooperation. Listen carefully to what he or she says and be open to learning and changing. Restate each other's positions.

4. Agree on the problem. Summarize the various viewpoints and state clearly the problem that you and the other group members think needs to be solved. Once all agree on this, focus on developing a solution.

5. Explore a range of possible solutions. Summarize points of agreement and disagreement. Look for creative alternatives.

6. Agree on what each person needs to do to solve the problem. Define the criteria for success with the following statement: "I will know this conflict is resolved to my satisfaction when . . ." Every group member needs to accept responsibility for making the team work.

Lesson Plans for Teaching Writing edited by Chris Jennings Dixon © 2007 National Council of Teachers of English.

Figure 1.5

LESSON 12
FEEDBACK: CREATING ONLINE PEER GROUPS

Michele Marits

Purpose

- To encourage peer feedback and develop awareness of evaluative criteria

Preparation

The instructor uploads the Grading Criteria for Essays handout in Blackboard at the beginning of the semester and instructs students to comment on all first drafts for the required semester essays by writing three to five complete sentences for each category.

Note: Blackboard is a management program for putting teaching materials on the Internet. Components of the program include personalizing the Blackboard environment, editing tools, creating announcements and assignments, transferring files onto Blackboard, conducting online discussions, creating and managing online tests. A basic knowledge of Windows operating system and word processing skills is necessary. Before using Blackboard, Word may be used to introduce students to Track Changes.

To Access Track Changes:

1. Open the document you want to revise.
2. On the Tools menu, click Track Changes.
3. When the Track Change feature is enabled, TRK appears on the status bar at the bottom of your document. When you turn off change tracking, TRK is dimmed.
4. Make the changes you want by inserting, deleting, or moving text or graphics.
5. You can also change color and formatting that Word uses to mark changed text and graphics.

Props/Materials

- Grading Criteria for Essays (Figure 1.6)
- Teacher and student access to Blackboard

Process/Procedure

Instructor Feedback

- With first drafts, the instructor comments on the first two criteria (focus and organization) by sending students an email.

- With successive drafts, the instructor uses Track Changes in Word to identify other areas of concern (content, style, conventions, and usage). Track Changes is a feature in Word that inserts comment boxes in visually-appealing colors without changing the students' essays.

Peer Feedback

- Students select the draft that appears below theirs in their group's file exchange.

- Students upload their comments in a forum in their group so all members can read the feedback given on every member's essay.

Pointers or Pitfalls

Instructors need to monitor the quality of student feedback and, if necessary, ask students to revise their feedback according to the grading criteria for essays.

Ponderings

The peer feedback portion of this assignment works well if the instructor encourages students to elaborate in each of the five categories by clarifying her or his comments and/or by giving examples from a peer's draft.

Grading Criteria for Essays

Your instructor will use the following general guidelines in grading your essays.

Points on final drafts have a value that can be converted to a numerical and letter system.

A (90–100 percent): This writing has the following characteristics:

- Focus: The writing has a clearly stated purpose that addresses the writing task in a thoughtful manner.
- Organization: The content is well organized with effective transitions and effective beginning and ending paragraphs.
- Content: Ideas are logical and fully developed through explanations, examples, evidence and/or other means appropriate to the assignment. Paragraphs are structured effectively.
- Style: The writer uses appropriate and precise word choices; language and sentence structure are alive, mature, and varied.
- Conventions and Usage: The writing contains no spelling errors and no conventional (mechanical) and usage errors. Control of diction is superior.

B (80–89 percent): The writing has the following characteristics:

- Focus: The writing effectively addresses the writing task and shows depth.
- Organization: The content is generally well organized with appropriate transitions and relevant beginning and ending paragraphs.
- Content: The content is adequately and thoughtfully developed with specific details, examples, evidence, etc.
- Style: The writer demonstrates facility with language, a mature range of vocabulary, and control of sentence-level style.
- Conventions and Usage: The writing contains no spelling errors and/or few conventional (mechanical) and usage errors.

C (70–79 percent): The writing has the following characteristics:

- Focus: The writing addresses the writing task but may lack complexity.
- Organization: The content shows some signs of logical organization with a beginning, middle, and end and some use of transitions.
- Content: The content is partially developed with some details, examples, evidence, etc. Paragraphing is appropriate.
- Style: The writer uses language adequately but with some imprecise word choice. The writing demonstrates some sentence variety.

Figure 1.6

Figure 1.6 continued

- Conventions and Usage: The writing contains a few spelling errors and/ or a few conventional (mechanical) and usage errors that do not inter- fere with meaning.

D (60–69 percent): The writing has the following characteristics:

- Focus: The writing has an inconsistent sense of purpose with a loose relation to the writing task.
- Organization: The content is inadequately organized and may have abrupt or illogical shifts and ineffective flow of ideas.
- Content: The content is incompletely developed and may be vague, sim- plistic, or stereotypical.
- Style: The writer uses inappropriate, imprecise, or inadequate language. Sentence variety is limited.
- Conventions and Usage: The writing contains repeated weaknesses in spelling, conventions (mechanics), and usage. Patterns of errors may be present.

F (50 percent of point value): The writing has the following characteristics:

- Focus: The writing has a confused sense of purpose and/or no evidence of connection to the writing task.
- Organization: The organization is confusing. The writing contains no transitions; the beginning and ending do not relate to the content.
- Content: The content is superficially developed and contains inadequate, inappropriate, or redundant details. Paragraphing is inadequate.
- Style: The writer uses inadequate and simplistic language. There are er- rors in word choice, and there is little or no sentence variety.
- Conventions and Usage: The writing contains repeated weaknesses in spelling, conventions (mechanics), and usage that interfere with the writer's purpose.

F (0 points): The writing does not address the basic criteria of the assign- ment.

- The writer submits writing that fails to address the basic requirements of the assignment.
- The writer submits drafts more than one week past the due date of the assignment.
- The writer intentionally plagiarizes.

Lesson Plans for Teaching Writing edited by Chris Jennings Dixon © 2007 National Council of Teachers of English.

LESSON 13
DEALER PREP: ALLEVIATING THE PAINS OF PEER EDITING

Thomas J. Hargrove

Purpose

- To develop accountability in the editing stage of composition

Preparation

No special preparation is needed beyond carefully explaining not only what students are going to be doing but why and, to a lesser extent, how. Students are accustomed to receiving notes and comments on their papers from their instructors. Learning how to edit themselves is a new, and often difficult, task students must master, i.e., moving beyond "This is good stuff" and "I really liked what you said." The challenge is to convince students that they are not through when they have finished writing their papers. "Dealer Prep"—making their work readable and credible to an audience on its own—is often more time consuming than the initial writing; however, it is more critical to successful essay presentation.

Props/Materials

- Drafts of written assignments in various stages of development
- Evaluation Criteria Checklist (Figure 1.7)

Process/Procedure

To provide focus and direction in peer-editing activities, the Evaluation Criteria Checklist is introduced. It is a compilation of the normal flaws often found in student work. Its unique feature is the parallel listing of what is good alongside what needs improvement or correction. After students become comfortable with working on each other's documents, I introduce using Track Changes (a Microsoft Word tool). This introduces accountability into the editing process since it tracks who did what and when. This tool also forces the author of a paper to consciously decide to accept or reject each suggested change.

Pointers or Pitfalls

Students are used to correcting their work after the instructor grades and returns it. They are not used to correcting the work of fellow students. At first, they are often hesitant to correct another's work. Many times, they are familiar with the terms and writing theory involved but lack practical experience in application. It is easier to learn how to detect errors in a written piece when it is someone else's work. It is even easier to just leave it to the teacher. This "natural resistance" has to be overcome.

Ponderings

I have found that it is easier to start by having students point out the good points in each other's work. They tend to be more detailed and specific in their comments when they are being positive. The Evaluation Criteria Checklist gives them a fairly comprehensive collection of points to look for. I started using Track Changes (and its Word Perfect equivalent) as an instructor's editing and feedback tool during spring 2005. It was so effective that I began using it as a peer-editing tool. If students are using MS Word or Word Perfect peer editing, a significant enhancement is potentially available. Both have tools for tracking changes (Word) and reviewers (Word Perfect). These are excellent feedback mechanisms for providing instructor feedback because they are done within the student's actual text. It works well for peer-editing exercises since it forces editors to write comments and suggestions. These tools provide the author, the editor, and the instructor with a clear picture of how a given assignment matures.

Note: This can work as a review checklist for a student's own work and for that of group mates when doing peer review. I've taken the standard "points off for" grading sheet and tried to translate it into a good text—bad text checklist.

Evaluation Criteria Checklist: Two Sides of the Equation

ORGANIZATION
[*positive*]
- Introduction and conclusion are well suited to the essay.
- Paragraphs are unified (all information supports one idea).
- There is a logical sequence of information.
- Writer makes smooth transitions between and within paragraphs.
- Writer demonstrates effective use of organizational modes.

[*negative*]
Introduction:
- Lacks an introduction:
  -No clear thesis statement.
  -No plan for intended development.
Body:
- Lacks coherence within
  -Paragraph
  -Essay
- Fails to logically present ideas.
- Lacks effective paragraphing.
- Contains extraneous material.
Conclusion:
- Lacks a conclusion.
- Fails to restate thesis statement to conclude.

CONTENT
- Essay accomplishes task set by assignment.
- There is a clear, precise, purpose/central idea.
- Essay is well focused.
- Assertions are supported by verifiable facts, details, examples, and illustrations.
- Essay is appropriate for the chosen audience.

- Fails to explain ideas presented.
- Lacks specific details.
- Lacks transitions within paragraphs.
- Fails to address thesis.
- Lacks substance.
- Fails to write on assigned topic.
- Essay is too short (less than XXX words).
- Essay is too long (more than YYY words).

DICTION
- Word choice is clear and precise.
- Writer uses few colloquialisms and cliches.
- There is no wordiness or redundancy.
- Writer uses strong verbs, strong nouns, predominantly active voice.
- (Optional) Writer uses metaphor and analogy effectively.

- Lack of Audience Awareness:
  -Style shifts
  -Point of view shifts
- Poor Word Choice:
  -Clichés
  -Wordiness/redundancy
  -Vagueness
  -Omitted words
  -Nonstandard/inappropriate word usage

Figure 1.7

Figure 1.7 continued

SENTENCE STRUCTURE
- Writer makes no run-ons or comma splices.
- Writer uses no inappropriate fragments.
- Writer uses properly placed modifiers.
- Writer varies sentence length and structure patterns.
- Writer uses unambiguous pronouns, including this and it.

- Misused sentence fragments.
- Run-on sentences.
- Comma splices.
- Out-of-control/unclear structures.
- Misplaced adjectival phrases.
- Too many short sentences.
- Lacking sentence variety.

MECHANICS
- Writer shows agreement between subjects and verbs, pronouns and antecedents.
- Writer is consistent in point of view, number, tense, and case.
- Writer uses correct spelling and capitalization.

- Errors in Spelling:
  -Spelling
  -Homonym
  -Split-word
- Improper Usage:
  -Verb forms
  -Noun forms
  -Subject-verb agreement
  -Adjective/adverb forms
  -Pronoun case agreement
  -Pronoun antecedent agreement
  -Unclear pronoun reference
  -Capitalization
- Punctuation Errors
  -End marks
  -Commas
  -All others

Lesson Plans for Teaching Writing edited by Chris Jennings Dixon © 2007 National Council of Teachers of English.

LESSON 14
"IT'S MUSIC TO MY EARS": GROWING PARAGRAPHS INTO ESSAYS

Thomas J. Hargrove

Purpose

- To construct essays from paragraphs using external sources

Preparation

This is a composition class exercise that can be used fairly early in a course. This assignment is intended to teach essay building and the use of external sources. It is preceded by a paragraph-level assignment in which students write about a favorite type of music and explain why they like it. Their individual music paragraphs are posted to a class discussion board for everyone to see. Each student then collects at least two paragraphs written by classmates.

Props/Materials

- It's Music to My Ears handout (Figure 1.8)
- Instructor and student use of computers
- Posting instructions as an assignment in Blackboard
- Setting up a discussion board for students to post their works in progress and their completed work

Note: Although I work in a computer classroom, this activity can be adapted for any teaching environment.

Process/Procedure

Students start with three paragraphs written by three different students. They must revise these paragraphs so that they sound as if they come from one voice. The process ends with each student composing a traditional five-paragraph essay—one paragraph at a time.

Pointers or Pitfalls

In itself, this appears to be a fairly simplistic exercise. However, it is another training session in basic content organization for presentation to an audience. It introduces using source materials and adapting them for the student's own purposes. As such, it represents a practical content development tool when understood and applied consistently. If students become confused as the assignment progresses, guide them individually to compare and contrast the content in given paragraphs.

Ponderings

The choice of topic—personal musical tastes—is an easy one for most students to write about. They all have favorites. Comparing and contrasting three different sets of musical preferences occurs with little need for instructor prompting and leads to interesting and active class discussion. Many students are surprised to find they have written a complete essay with relatively no pain.

It's Music to My Ears

This assignment is intended to help you practice several different aspects of written communication. First, we need to agree on some new vocabulary; not just as words, but as tools.

Background
Paragraphs are similar to sentences in that they are designed to deal with one point or idea at a time (one thought, maybe?). They just deal with bigger points and ideas. While they don't have the same set of grammatical labels as sentences for identifying problems such as fragments and run-ons (too little or too much), they do have the same problems. So we are going to borrow a few labels.

We will have "paragraph fragments" when what looks like a paragraph doesn't completely develop a thought. The fix is to revise and expand the paragraph to create a complete thought package; revise it for inclusion in an existing paragraph or simple elimination. Elimination represents a decision that the partial thought doesn't fit in, or fit in at this point. The solution will be driven by your message and what you are trying to do with it. If it supports the mission but doesn't do it well, revise. If it doesn't support it, delete.

We will have "run-on paragraphs" when more than one complete thought is present. If there are two complete thought packages, we have a fused paragraph. The fix is to break it into separate paragraphs for each thought. If we have more than one completely developed thought but not really two, the extra material has to be reworked. This could involve rewriting for inclusion in the now expanded original paragraph; deleting it as unnecessary; or, rewriting and expanding it into a separate paragraph. Once again, the solution will be driven by your message and what you are trying to do with it.

Now, the assignment:

1. Your first paragraph is a stand alone explanation of one type of music you enjoy and why you enjoy it. There is a discussion board forum set up for this assignment. Post your paragraph there and read the other postings to see what others think is good music.

2. Using copies of two other paragraphs written by your classmates, construct an essay in the basic five-paragraph mode: introduction, body one, body two, body three, conclusion. But you can't simply put the three paragraphs you have together and tack on an introduc-

Figure 1.8

Figure 1.8 continued

tion and a conclusion. Why not? The paragraphs you have are independent constructions by different authors. The actual number of body paragraphs will depend on how many paragraphs you have to start with and how you decide to use them. For example, if two people both like the same music, you might consider discussing them both at the same time. (More than five paragraphs is always acceptable, of course.)

3. This is your essay, so you have to write it. You should retain and accurately reflect the thoughts of all authors you use. However, you have to revise them so that the resulting text is your own and reflects who you are as a writer with your unique style. You are the one writing your essay.

4. Your own paragraph and those of your group mates are your raw material. How you design and build your essay is up to you. The normal way to approach this would be to use comparison and contrast; using your musical tastes as your base for discussing similarities and differences.

5. You can use the material in the different paragraphs almost as written. You will need to change some of the phrasings since you are the one doing the talking. One simple way to introduce another person's position would be: "Tamika says . . ." "Tamika's favorite music is . . ." "While I like . . . Stephanie prefers . . ."

6. Your introduction introduces yourself and your intentions in the following discussion. It reflects your basic position on good music. The body of your essay grows from your three core paragraphs. You need to interconnect them. At a minimum, you need to ensure that you have smooth transitions from one paragraph to the next. Using more substantive linkages, such as parallel treatment of points within and between the paragraphs, is a definite plus.

7. Your conclusion will recap where you are coming from and request that your readers consider reassessing their views about music based on what you have said.

Lesson Plans for Teaching Writing edited by Chris Jennings Dixon © 2007 National Council of Teachers of English.

LESSON 15
CREATING PULLOUTS: ENHANCING ESSAYS

Elizabeth H. Beagle

Purpose

- To create eye-catching pullouts to enhance essays and emphasize major points

Preparation

Students need access to computers; therefore, schedule time for the class in a computer lab. Conduct a mini-lesson on how to create text boxes using Microsoft Word. (See Figure 1.9.)

Props/Materials

Provide practice exercises using Drawing and Text Box features in Word and reserve access to computers.

Process/Procedure

1. Students must have written a rough draft of any type of essay already.
2. Students peruse magazines and newspapers to identify

Creating Text Boxes

1. On the **Drawing** toolbar, click **Text Box** ▣. (A toolbar is a bar with buttons and options that you use to carry out commands. To display a toolbar, click Customize on the Tools menu and then click the Toolbars tab.)
2. Click in your document (or drag the icon to) where you want to insert the text box. (A text box is a movable, resizable container for text or graphics. Use text boxes to position several blocks of text on a page or to give text a different orientation from other text in the document.)

You can use the options on the **Drawing** toolbar to enhance a text box. For example, change the fill color—just as you can with any other drawing.

Figure 1.9

use of pullouts and to note how they are used to provoke interest in reading the entire article.

3. Provide practice in creating text boxes or pullouts.

4. Assign students to create three pullouts for their selected essay.

5. In small groups, have students review the use of pullouts and comment upon the effectiveness of this technique.

Pointers or Pitfalls

Students should be told that the pullout is not actually "pulled out" of the essay. Demonstrate how magazines, newspapers, etc. use pullouts as hooks. Also, ensure that students have thought about the most effective pullouts and where to place them strategically within the body of the essay.

Ponderings

This is a great way to get students to think about and demonstrate the focus of their essays.

LESSON 16
YOUR PAPER: IMPROVING PERSUASIVE WRITING

Ramona Clark

Purpose

- To improve a persuasive essay with guided directions
- To analyze the accuracy, relevance, and organization of evidence

Preparation

Prepare the students for this activity by reviewing the elements of argumentation in writing a persuasive essay. Sequential steps of persuasion/argument should include: (1) choose a position or side of an issue or problem, (2) understand the opposite viewpoint of your position and counter it, (3) provide specific and convincing evidence that appeals to reason, (4) structure your essay to convey purpose and topic using examples that enhance meaning, (5) conclude your argument with a strong statement that reinforces the points you have made and suggests future action.

Props/Materials

- Improving a Persuasive Paper handout (Figure 1.10)

Process/Procedure

Assign students to read the student sample paper on the handout; then they are to pretend that they have written the paper. Students need to respond to the questions on the handout and revise the sample as if the paper is theirs. They are to hand in their revisions. In small groups, students may then discuss and review their individual responses and compare and contrast techniques.

Pointers or Pitfalls

Students need adequate background in persuasive techniques. Assigning the work to be done as a quiz grade may be needed to motivate the reluctant learner.

Ponderings

In general, students do very well with this exercise. They respond well to the guided nature of this assignment.

Improving a Persuasive Paper

Read the following student sample paper and then answer questions 1–8, pretending that this is your paper. Revise according to the directions below.

Sample Student Paper

(1) Why do they have to treat us like children? Their plan is really bad. Why can't we make up our own minds about what we do with our own time? This really makes me mad.

(2) Besides, suppose you got sick or something. Or suppose you broke a leg. It's not the same thing as cutting classes.

(3) If I miss classes, I'm already getting punished because I have to make up the work anyway, and I might not get as good grades on my test because I missed stuff in class, and anyway some teachers give you a zero in class if you don't raise your hand a lot, so my grade would get lowered anyway. My grade in English got lowered last year because this kid kept talking to me and passing me notes and I didn't want him to. And if I'm willing to accept those consequences and still get a passing grade, why should the system make me lose credit for the course.

(4) One of the things we're supposed to learn in school is how to be responsible. So we need to make our own decisions, or we'll never learn how.

1. Can my reader tell what the issue is and how the writer feels about it from the way the paper begins? What do "they," "really bad," and "this" refer to in paragraph 1? (If you don't know, no one else will, either.) Discuss the meaning of the words and then rewrite the paragraph.
2. Is paragraph 2 complete? Does the reader know what the writer is referring to? Is the transition word accurate? Add additional details.
3. In paragraph 2, the writer says, "It's not the same thing as cutting class." Has the writer really responded to the point of view of the other side? What should the writer add? Write the additional sentence or sentences.
4. Paragraph 3 begins with a sentence that is too long and difficult to read: "If I miss classes, I'm already getting punished. . . ." Break the sentence into two or more separate sentences and write the new paragraph.
5. What reasons support the writer's opinion? Write the reasons. Are each of the reasons supported? If not, what examples could you use from your own experience to support each reason? Write your examples or details here.
6. As the writer, do I need to give another reason for rejecting the attendance policy? If so, what sentence or sentences need to be added? What facts, details, or examples can you supply? Write the new sentences here as a paragraph with a main idea and supporting details.
7. Does this paper sound angry or calm? Is it respectful of the opposition? Identify the words that make the tone inappropriate and rewrite these sentences using different word choices.
8. As the writer, have I ended by stating what I want to happen or by suggesting an action? How could I improve my ending? Write the new ending.

Lesson Plans for Teaching Writing edited by Chris Jennings Dixon © 2007 National Council of Teachers of English.

Figure 1.10

LESSON 17
EVERYBODY'S A STUDENT AND EVERYBODY'S A TEACHER: REFLECTING UPON KNOWLEDGE

David Meyerholz

Purpose

- To reflect and analyze personal connections to classroom content

Preparation

Begin by asking students to brainstorm in writing what has been most important to them in their class studies. Suggested prompts: (1) What topics or issues did you find the most interesting? (2) How do you think this topic or issue will affect you in your future endeavors? Ask students to fold a piece of notebook paper in half lengthwise and to make two lists—one on the left side for issues or topics of personal interest (this one will be the longest) and one on the right explaining personal connections (this one might take more prompting). Ultimately, students are directed to pick an area for further investigation from their lists.

Note: Here are two examples from my government class of sample topics, the students' connections, and the follow-up study:

- First example: Topic—"Unemployment in America" with student connection— "Get a better paying job" followed by—"Explore opportunities for employment at the VA Employment Center."
- Second example: Topic—"Personal Legal Rights" with student connection—"What happens when I go to court for a speeding ticket?" followed by— "Invite a policeman or defense attorney to class."

In English classes, topics may be developed using conflicts and/or themes from literary works.

Props/Materials

Students must verbalize their newfound knowledge with the assistance of visual cues, and they must be able to respond to reasonable questions from their peers and teacher.

Process/Procedure

Provide a suggested timeline for the entire process:

- Brainstorming Session—up to two weeks
- Discovery Period—two to three weeks
- Presentations—allow fifteen minutes for each student
- Reflection—typed paper in which students reflect on what they have learned and where they might go from here.

You should expect some students to change their minds about what they're investigating. As most writing is rewriting, much thinking should be rethinking. The "discovery" part of this task does not have to be prolonged, but it should be documented. I also require that this phase include interaction with a live human being, who either serves as an authority on the topic or gives an additional perspective about the subject under investigation.

Students must plan a fifteen-minute presentation on what they have learned. Presentations may include Power Point shows, guest speakers (in activities where students still take an active role), home-made videos, and other interactive formats involving the student audience, for example—a student version of *Survival*. To conclude this activity, students must reflect on their work by evaluating the experience and pondering how they can further pursue this area of interest.

Pointers or Pitfalls

I have found it doesn't work to cram all of these presentations into a set period of time. Instead, it works well for me to intersperse them with other planned activities. "Type A" teachers who need to have every minute planned three months in advance should disregard my previous suggestion.

Ponderings

I'm probably no different from most teachers in that there are times when I'm presenting a lesson plan that seems to be going exceedingly well, and I'll think, "Damn, I'm good!" Except, how do we really know that all of the young people on the other end are receiving the lesson in the same world-class way in which we are giving it?

I find that, despite my patient and well-reasoned approach, more than a few students do not share with me the same sense of importance over much of the subject matter in my courses. We can pretend this doesn't exist and go about our business as usual, or maybe we take this reality and turn it into an opportunity.

We should be accessing out students' perceptions of relevance and connecting them with lessons in our curriculum. While I can't come close to claiming this activity is a success with 100 percent of my students, I can say that in intervening years more than a few have recalled this activity as extremely worthwhile. It does reinforce learning as a lifelong process.

LESSON 18
APPLICATION/SCHOLARSHIP: WRITING A PERSONAL ESSAY

Joseph H. Lemrow

Purpose

- To write a personal essay for application to a college or for financial assistance

Preparation

Ask students to take a personal inventory by stepping outside of themselves to determine those qualities others see in them that suggest persistence, leadership ability, dedication to specific tasks, and/or promise of success. Because of the difficulty of evaluating oneself, encourage students to ask friends, relatives, and former and present teachers for their impressions.

Props/Materials

Provide a handout with questions related to three broad categories:

1. **Academics**
   Were you ever on the dean's list?
   Did you earn any academic awards?
   Were you a member of an honor society?
   Did you belong to any clubs or organizations?
   What was your grade point average?
   What was your standing in your class?

Did you excel in the arts, in the sciences, in the social sciences? Other areas?

2. **Community Involvement/Volunteerism**
   Have you been active in church-related activities?
   Have you volunteered at a local hospital?
   Did you volunteer time/effort toward the completion of a community project (for example, Habitat for Humanity)?
   Have you worked with the elderly?
   Did you coach/train young people?
   Have you worked to improve the environment?
   Were you active in any political campaigns?

3. **Work-Related Experience**
   Have you acquired any marketable skills on the job?
   Were you given additional responsibilities by an employer?
   Did your supervisor recognize your leadership skills?
   Were you placed in charge of any project?
   Did your employer recognize your work habits/job skills?

Process/Procedure

1. **Essay Openings**
   Suggest students begin their essays by telling who they are and why they are writing. That is, mention the name of the college or group to whom they are writing and explain short- and long-term goals. These goals need to be clearly expressed. They may also explain what courses of study they intend to pursue or what degrees they intend to obtain. Students should try to create thesis statements that indicate what subcategories are intended to be discussed in the content paragraphs. They should strive to write an opening of three to five sentences.

2. **Middle Paragraph Strategies**
   Students write separate paragraphs (however brief) for each of the categories (academics, volunteerism, and work experience). They do not merely list; rather, they explain what these experiences tell about them.

3. **Summaries**
   Students write summaries, not conclusions, reminding the reader of their short- and long-term goals. They should stress what steps

they have taken to achieve their goals. They may mention how one or two skills have contributed to their achievements. Remind students to be aware of an audience, since a committee will usually judge who will be admitted to a college or determine who will be awarded scholarship monies. Finally, students should exit gracefully in their conclusions and tell the college or group that they will make them proud to have supported them.

Pointers or Pitfalls

Ask students to write with a degree of verve! They should show their personality and, above all, use strong, dynamic, descriptive verbs. Remind them to always mention the college or institution by name and to avoid the impression that they may be writing a generic statement to be sent to many groups. Moreover, they should be cautioned not to mention the word *money.* Instead, prompt them to use phrases like "invest in my future," or "support my efforts."

Ponderings

The aim of this activity is for students to write the sort of essay many colleges and universities require as part of an admissions package from prospective students or the sort of essay that may be used to ask a corporation or group for financial assistance to further their studies. Moreover, this activity can be modified for an application for employment by including a cover letter and resume.

LESSON 19
COLLEGE EXPLORATION: WRITING AN EXPOSITORY REPORT

Miles McCrimmon

Purpose

- To research objective source materials
- To prepare an expository report demonstrating understanding of rhetorical modes

Preparation

Spend some class time surveying college websites in a computer classroom. Ask your career/transfer advisors and counselors to contribute the latest pile of mailings from colleges. The tactile experience of looking at brochures is still helpful. Get your students comfortable with the Aristotelian appeals (logos, ethos, mythos, and pathos) used by colleges. Also look at some examples of college admissions and scholarship application essays and prompts.

Note: For students who are not college minded, this activity may be adapted for a career search using job-related materials.

Props/Materials

- College websites, brochures, and applications
- College Exploration Assignment handout (Figure 1.11)

Process/Procedure

See the College Exploration Assignment handout for an outline of the three-step process. The entire assignment should take no more than four weeks. Students research materials to create a presentation of themselves for college or employer to determine their candidacy.

Step 1: Analysis of the college or university's image

Step 2: Personal statement

Step 3: Recap of strategies

Pointers or Pitfalls

Because I work with community college freshmen, many of whom are the first in their family to attend college, I frequently use higher education as a central site of analysis. This assignment works even better with my college-bound dual-enrolled high school seniors. For those of my students who are already seriously involved in the workforce, or who soon will be, I have developed a variation of this assignment that focuses on employers.

Ponderings

The application and scholarship essays I would otherwise be asked to critique for free I am now able to include as part of a graded assignment. Of course, the websites accessed in these assignments, whether from colleges, corporations, or the military, present ready opportunities to discuss audience, purpose, and context, as well as principles of visual rhetoric.

College Exploration Assignment

If you are planning to attend a four-year college or university in the near future, you might be interested in choosing this assignment. This project takes the form of an expository report that will have three parts. While Parts 1 and 3 are more private—not to be seen by the college—Part 2 should be composed as a public document.

You will research a college or university that you are personally interested in attending. You may even be on your way there; if so, you may want to pretend you haven't been accepted yet. Using materials from your chosen college's websites, mailings, advertisements, brochures, and/or tours, study the image that the college is trying to portray about its campus and faculty, its students and student life, and its academics and even its athletics. Also, using some reliably objective resources, gather and review some basic facts about your chosen college.

Part 1 should be an analysis of the college's or university's image, with a special focus on any discrepancies between facts you have gathered independently about the college (from the *U.S. News & World Report* rankings, for example) and claims the college makes for itself in its own marketing. As you address how the college presents itself to its public constituencies (parents, students, alumni, faculty and staff, state legislatures/governors, boards of trustees), analyze its use of the four rhetorical appeals (logos, ethos, mythos, and pathos). See glossary of terms below.

Part 2 should be a "Personal Statement" of the type one frequently sees on college applications. You should write your personal statement honestly but with an eye toward what you have learned in your research about the type of student profile your chosen institution appears to desire. Try to balance the tasks of self-promotion required by this unique genre (establishment of ethos, evidence of potential academic productivity, etc.). If you would like to use an essay prompt from an actual application, feel free.

Part 3 should be a brief recap of the strategies you used in the personal statement to make yourself an attractive candidate for admission.

Glossary of Terms

Logos: facts, statistics, logic, reason

Pathos: emotions (usually hope or fear or some derivation thereof)

Ethos: the company's own credibility, reputation, tradition, trustworthiness

Mythos: commonly shared cultural beliefs like patriotism and religion

(This activity can be adapted to use with an industry search and employee application.)

Lesson Plans for Teaching Writing edited by Chris Jennings Dixon © 2007 National Council of Teachers of English.

Figure 1.11

LESSON 20
THE FINAL WORD IS YOURS: ASSESSING THE CLASSROOM EXPERIENCE

David Meyerholz

Purpose

- To reflect upon and assess classroom experiences using constructive criticism

Preparation

After running into and reminiscing with more and more former students, I became increasingly convinced that some formal writing assignment should end the school year (and, for seniors, their high school careers) that brings their educational experiences into some kind of perspective. I, therefore, designed the writing assignment that follows to conclude the academic careers of most of my students. This is an end-of-the-year assignment, so preparation is having students get to this point.

Props/Materials

None; this is not an assignment to be researched or presented in advance.

Process/Procedure

I begin by expressing my hope that the school year has been educational and at least somewhat enjoyable. Then I direct that the last assignment is to review the year in a one-page *typed* paper in which students answer the following questions:

1. What subject matter (or topic) did you find the most and least interesting?

2. How could the class have been run better, and what did you like about it?

3. How do you think your experience in this class is most likely to affect you in your future endeavors?

4. What recommendations can you make about the focus, methodology, and teaching style for future classes?

Note: I reinforce that I'm interested in constructive criticism and not in pandering (we should leave that to the politicians). Students are encouraged just to be thorough and honest.

Pointers or Pitfalls

The paper must be typed. Besides making the paper more readable, typing also lends a more formal and dignified air to the student's thoughts. (And it's a requirement in my class for most take-home writing anyway.) I do allow the papers to be anonymous. As each student hands in the work, a quick glance to see that it is the approximate one to two pages in length and, bingo, the student gets a 100 percent in the grade book. Some students are going to be more thoughtful than others, but I'm convinced you gain far more than you lose by allowing some students the comfort of expressing honest thoughts most completely. Besides, less than half choose anonymity anyway.

Ponderings

These papers are absolutely a treat to read. It's not because they are glowingly full of praise; on the contrary, high school students in June are quite willing to express the full range of their opinions. The professional teacher should be ready to embrace this and come back the next year even better!

LESSON 21
"HANDS OFF": ROLE MODELING THE READER/WRITER RELATIONSHIP

Chris Jennings Dixon

Purpose

- To learn about the writing process from the perspective of reader/consultant
- To practice reader/writer interaction strategies
- To develop skill in listening to analyze communication

Preparation

Prior to the role-modeling experience, students prepare a first draft of a writing assignment to use for the reader/writer activity. Inform students that they will be exposed to the values of reader/consultant through a presentation of tutorial strategies in a role modeling practice.

Props/Materials

- Writing handbook

Process/Procedure

1. The teacher divides the class into triads. Each student has written a first draft.

2. The teacher instructs students to introduce themselves and talk for a few minutes about the writing assignment that prompted their drafts.

3. The teacher guides students to offer assistance to members of the group by listening to readings of selected works and making general responses that encourage the writer to revise the work.

4. Throughout this activity, the teacher monitors group work by walking around the classroom and encouraging students to follow the prescribed behaviors.

5. Taking turns, each student orally reads his or her draft aloud to the group.

6. As each writer reads, the other students listen without pencils in their hands and concentrate on remembering two items: (1) strengths in the paper (2) areas that need further elaboration

7. Following each reading, student listeners thank the writer for sharing the draft.

8. Each listener relates at least one strength in the paper for the writer to note. Dialogue ensues among the group, detailing how the strength fortifies the draft.

9. Each listener relates an area that needs further elaboration for the writer to follow up on. Dialogue ensues among the group about possible ways to add to the draft.

10. After each reading, the listeners formulate questions for the writer about the draft, such as "Here is what I heard is your position on _____, is that accurate? If not, what is it? If so, I understand your reason for your position is _____. Is that right?" The group discusses what has been heard from the listener/reader's point of view and what was attempted from the writer's point of view.

11. If a writer asks a specific technical question about grammar or mechanics, the group members assist the student in looking up information in a writing handbook and applying rules to the item in question.

12. To provide a finale for the experience, the teacher brings the class back to a general discussion of what and how they experienced in the role playing.

13. Using student feedback, the teacher develops a "Do and Don't" list for the reader/writer relationship on the board.

Pointers or Pitfalls

Students need to practice and reflect upon the roles of tutor and tutee to understand the emotional background that may be part of the experience of sharing one's work in progress. Students should maintain a "hands off" mode of approaching another student's work. They need to be cautioned not to provide writing instruction nor to correct or "fix" writing problems. The emphasis in the tutorial experience should be on oral reading and discussion of a work with student reader/listeners offering a live audience but no specific feedback. The reader may re-phrase the writer's work to help the writer clarify what he or she intended to say.

If a high school writing center has been established, students may volunteer as consultants and continue their training as tutors. Developing an open environment for reflection upon writing and supporting student writing are two important features of the writing center experience. Ideally, student consultants should have opportunities to share their perception about tutoring with each other. A Writing Center Club may be another good venue for this activity.

Ponderings

Students who have found merit in the reader/writer relationship may be encouraged to volunteer as student consultants for a high school writing center. The writing center coordinator can provide additional training and ongoing support for those students.

To adequately staff a high school writing center, it is often necessary to obtain student volunteers to assist teachers. At first, motivating students to participate in a student-reader relationship may require tangible carrots, such as extra credit. However, once students experience the consultant role, they find that they have learned more about their own writing processes. Students are often energized by writing center experiences and continue to use writing center resources in college. Additionally, students who have participated as consultants in high school writing centers often decide to pursue educational careers.

II Portfolios

"Why portfolios?" Focusing on assignments that encourage self-reflection and revision, teachers can adapt already required writing folders to the portfolio model. The portfolio model alters the evidence or demonstration approach of simply gathering samples of student work to one that organically provides examples of student improvement via pre-, ongoing, and post-composition for an outside reader's assessment. Throughout the process, students are prompted to reflect on their growth as writers, to develop an understanding of their unique strengths and weaknesses in composition, and to revise their work. Encouraging and providing opportunities for students to focus on what they can do well through reflective and self-assessment strategies, teachers cast off traditional approaches to editing and grading papers. This section provides samples of activities that have been effective for both classroom and institutional portfolio programs. Additionally, several of the lessons utilize computer technology as an optional format for student portfolios. In these lessons, the teacher-contributors offer practical insights into teaching and learning with the Internet.

LESSON 22
FIRST IMPRESSIONS: CREATING REFLECTIVE LETTERS

Shanita Williams

Purpose

- To reflect on personal writing experiences

Preparation

Begin by discussing the purpose of collecting works in a progress folder. Encourage students to be aware of the correlation between our life experiences and our writing. The reflective letter is written at the beginning of the year and stored in students' progress folders until the end on the year. The students will use these letters as tools to reflect upon the changes in their lives and in their writing. Explain to the students that they will write reflective essays at the end of the year, and these letters will help them see changes in their lives and writing.

Props/Materials

Envelopes and folders for collecting student work

Process/Procedure

1. The teacher instructs students to be specific and provide details in one-page letters to themselves answering the following questions:
   - What are your first impressions of your new teachers and classes?
   - What is happening in your life (boyfriend/girlfriend, family, friends, activities, etc.)?
   - What do you hope to achieve in English this year?
2. The teacher assures the students that NO ONE, including the teacher, will read the letters.
3. As students complete their letters, they fold the letters and place them into envelopes. The students seal the envelopes and sign their names across the seal.
4. Students self-address the letters and place their envelopes into their progress folders.

5. The teacher returns the envelopes/letters to the students at the end of the year.

6. As a culminating activity, the teacher assigns students to write reflective essays using materials from their earlier letters to reflect upon their growth.

Pointers or Pitfalls

It is helpful for students to hear a reading of a teacher-prepared sample prior to writing their own letters. Because the teacher will not be reading the student letters, it is advisable to monitor student work by walking around the classroom and encouraging students to stay on task during the activity.

Ponderings

This activity establishes a high level of trust in the classroom as students learn that they can write for themselves in a protected environment.

LESSON 23
DEAR READER: SELF-ASSESSMENT AND REFLECTION

Frances G. Sharer

Purpose

- To recognize the role of reflection in the writing process
- To practice reflection for individual pieces of writing

Preparation

Start simply. Have the students respond to one question about their writing. They are usually most comfortable with writing a response/reflection about the process they use. Later, when they become more aware of the power of reflection, they are willing to do much more than discuss process.

Props/Materials

- Reflective Prompts handout (Figure 2.1)
- Ideas on Reflection handout (Figure 2.2)
- Prompts for Cover Notes handout (Figure 2.3)
- Reflective Letter handout (Figure 2.4)
- Self-Assessment/Reflection Strategies handout (Figure 2.5)
- Portfolio Final Reflection handout (Figure 2.6)

Process/Procedure

Work with handouts, prompts, and writing reflections to help students assess their works in progress as well as their final portfolios. Guide students to make honest assessments and reflections upon their writing. Students evolve in their understanding of the importance of examination and reflection upon their writing as they develop increased control of their writing process.

Pointers or Pitfalls

Start small. Students will readily discuss something they feel they did well. I always begin with the positive. Of course, I also ask students to reflect on choices for inclusion in their portfolios.

Ponderings

When I began with portfolios, I thought that reflection just might be the one most important mark of growth. After six years of working with portfolios, I am more convinced than ever that reflection is a key to successful writing.

Reflective Prompts

Select one of the following prompts to reflect on your writing experience.

1. Who are you as a learner, and who are you as a writer?

2. What do you already know about this topic?

3. Now that you have written on this topic, what did you learn?

4. Do you need to learn more? If so, what?

5. Use this opening: "I believe this is the best paper I have written, and I'll explain why."

6. Use this opening: "I doubt that this essay/paper is very good. The reason I say that is . . ."

7. Use this opening: "I predict my teacher's reaction to this paper will be . . . (comment, not a grade)."

8. Do you agree with the way a peer reader (or outside reader) has read your paper? Why or why not?

9. Use this opening: "I will remember this piece of writing twenty years from now because . . ."

10. When writing this paper, what did you discover about yourself?

Lesson Plans for Teaching Writing edited by Chris Jennings Dixon © 2007 National Council of Teachers of English.

Figure 2.1

Ideas on Reflection

Cognitive

Reflection on the learning associated with this piece of writing: is best if the learning is tied to a reading you have done during the learning process.

   EXAMPLES:
- Why do poets include figurative language in their writing? How have you used figurative language in your poem?
- What is the role of a conflict in a story? How did you develop your narrative around a conflict?

Reflection that focuses on the writer's revision of this piece.

   EXAMPLES:
- As we revised our essays, we focused on improving organization and unity through transitional devices and topic sentences. How did you change your topic sentences from the first draft to the final draft? What transitional words did you include and why did you select them?
- What was one goal you had for improving your writing? How did you change your first draft to achieve this goal?

Reflection that focuses on the writer's editing of this piece.

   EXAMPLES:
- How do you form and punctuate a compound sentence? How did you combine simple sentences from your first draft to form and punctuate compound sentences in your final draft? (Differentiation)
- What was one goal you had for editing your writing? How did you change your first draft to achieve this goal? (Differentiation)

Affective
- What was the hardest part of writing this piece?
- What is your favorite part of this piece?
- What section of the paper did you change the most from your first draft to your second draft?
- What was one suggestion made by a peer and how did you use the suggestion to improve your final draft?

Reflective Cover Letter for the Writing Portfolio (Affective)
- Which is your favorite piece in the portfolio? Why?
- Which piece best represents your growth as a writer? Why?
- Which piece still requires revision? Why?
- How has the portfolio helped to show who you are as a writer?
- What would you like the reader to know about you as a student and a writer?

Lesson Plans for Teaching Writing edited by Chris Jennings Dixon © 2007 National Council of Teachers of English.

Figure 2.2

**Prompts for Cover Notes When Selecting Pieces
for Inclusion in the Portfolio**

You may choose to include pieces of writing in your portfolio for a variety
of reasons. One piece may represent your best writing effort. Another may
show that you have mastered a new skill or experimented with a new style.
You may even choose to include a work just because you especially like it.
No matter what your reasons, it is helpful to write down why you selected
each piece and what that piece tells about you as a writer. The sentence start-
ers below can help you reflect on your choices.

- I chose to include this work because . . .

- I am proud of this work because . . .

- I chose to include this piece of writing to demonstrate how
  much I have improved at . . .

- I chose to include this piece of writing because it is my first
  attempt at . . .

- This work represents . . .

- I chose to include this piece of writing because it shows how
  my ideas developed into a final product. You can see how . . .

- It might be helpful for you to know that . . .

- I worked very hard to . . .

- The best part of this piece of writing is . . .

- One thing I hoped to achieve in this piece of writing was . . .

- One way I might try to improve this work is . . .

- For me, the hardest part of this assignment was . . .

- For me, the most enjoyable part of this assignment was . . .

- By working on this piece of writing, I learned . . .

- I used to think . . . , but now I know . . .

- It was difficult for me to learn . . .

- If I were to begin this work again, I would . . .

- The strongest element in this piece of writing is . . .

- At first, I was having trouble . . . , but then I . . .

Lesson Plans for Teaching Writing edited by Chris Jennings Dixon © 2007 National
Council of Teachers of English.

Figure 2.3

Reflective Letter

Directions: Your assignment is to write a reflective letter to me or a class-mate that answers and explains the following questions. Use the format of a friendly letter and begin with the salutation "Dear Reader." Remember the value of risk taking. Select and focus on different topics and ideas each time you reflect!

I.   What is reflection?
   A.   Reflection asks you to consider the following seven steps:
      1.   Know your work.
      2.   Like—find something you like.
      3.   Compare this experience to another writing experience.
      4.   Critique the product.
      5.   Evaluate your effort.
      6.   Connect to previous work and effort.
      7.   Project to the next project/effort.

II.   Possible ideas for your reflective letters:
      1.   What inspired you to write these pieces? How did you come to develop them?
      2.   What is the purpose of your piece? Who is your audience and why?
      3.   What do you especially like about your papers?
      4.   What gave you the most difficulty?
      5.   What did you learn about yourself as a writer during this process?
      6.   What goals did you achieve that you established early this year?
      7.   What do you consistently do well when you write?
      8.   What weaknesses do you often see?
      9.   Think of some great writers you've read. What do they do well in your opinion? How could you be like them or would you want to?
      10.   What kind of writer do you want to be in June?
      11.   What must you work on to achieve such goals?
      12.   Tell me something about this writing assignment that I don't already know.

Lesson Plans for Teaching Writing edited by Chris Jennings Dixon © 2007 National Council of Teachers of English.

Figure 2.4

Self-Assessment/Reflection Strategies

1. After each writing assignment, ask students to reflect on the process they went through in completing the tasks required and to express their opinions of their success. Ask them to quote their own favorite lines or paraphrase their best analogies or images or point out their successful incorporation of a grammar/mechanics concept the class studied recently.

2. As students hand in an assignment, give each of them a colored piece of paper and ask them to tell the teacher everything they want him/her to know about the problems, concerns, delights, and frustrations they experienced as they prepared this assignment. Then tell them to staple the sheet to either the front or the back of the paper depending on whether they want the teacher to have this "inside information" before reading the paper or after reading the paper. Of course, they must explain *why* they made this choice.

3. After encouraging students to share their prewritings and drafts with peers and/or family, ask them to talk about their experiences when they turn in the paper. Ask them to identify the most helpful pieces of information they received from a family member, peer, or friend. Ask them to identify something in their final paper that they chose NOT to change and tell why they made this decision.

4. Halfway through a writing task, ask students to outline the rest of their papers and to trade their papers (but not the outlines) with writing partners. Each partner finishes the paper and shares the results with the student writer. The two discuss the similar and different writing choices they made and the effectiveness of each piece.

5. After a few pieces have been added to the working portfolio, ask students to examine the contents and look for examples in their own words of grammatical concepts the class is discussing, such as an effective introduction or a vivid description. By having their works available to them at all times and by using them in a variety of ways, the students learn to use their previous experiences to sharpen new experiences (we hope).

Lesson Plans for Teaching Writing edited by Chris Jennings Dixon © 2007 National Council of Teachers of English.

Figure 2.5

Portfolio Final Reflection

Throughout the year, you have had the opportunity to reflect upon your growth as a writer. The reflection piece to be included in your portfolio is a letter to the reader(s) of your portfolio. In your letter, respond to the required prompts plus two others. You should look back through your portfolio to your previous reflections and writing pieces to gather ideas for this final reflection.

Required Prompts:

1. In what ways have you grown as a writer this year? Cite specific examples from your collection that show your growth.

2. Why did you select the "student choice" pieces that you included?

Optional Choice Prompts:

1. Look back at the first piece you wrote on your writing style. Of the weaknesses you mentioned, have any improved? If so, what is the reason for the improvement?

2. Select one or two of your remaining weaknesses in writing and outline a plan for improvement.

3. Where do you see yourself as a writer five years from now? Why?

4. Which piece is your favorite and why?

5. Which piece best represents your strengths as a writer?

6. Which piece is most distinctly "you"? Why?

7. Which piece was the most difficult for you? Why?

8. What important life lessons did you learn from your writing assignments?

9. What tools of revision, such as highlighting areas of concern, peer editing, teacher conferencing, or writing center visits, have worked the best for you and why? Do you have any other suggestions for editing tools?

10. If you were to pick one stage of the writing process (prewriting, writing, revising, editing, publishing), which is the most difficult for you? Which is the easiest?

Lesson Plans for Teaching Writing edited by Chris Jennings Dixon © 2007 National Council of Teachers of English.

Figure 2.6

LESSON 24
ROAD MAPS: DEVELOPING AN ANNOTATED TABLE OF CONTENTS

Frances G. Sharer

Purpose

- To develop and employ organizational devices for a Works in Progress folder or portfolio presentation

Preparation

Start a discussion of annotation with the first student writing assignment. After the student writer prepares each written piece, guide student in identification of the work by title or topic and due date. Then instruct students in writing individualized commentaries about their pieces.

Props/Materials

Sample Annotated Table of Contents handout (Figure 2.7)

Process/Procedure

As students produce more writing during the school year, they need to have a format for organizing their works in their progress folders/portfolios. Using an Annotated Table of Contents, students develop skills in identifying and organizing their cumulative writing experiences. The teacher can model a suggested format or use a model as a springboard to develop a customized format with the students. In addition to monitoring required writing pieces for inclusion in the portfolio, teachers need to guide students to provide a rationale for including selected pieces. Through the year and especially at the end of the academic period, these annotations enable students to reflect upon their progress as writers and help the readers of the portfolios recognize and assess student growth in writing.

Points or Pitfalls

Working from a necessity for organization of the portfolio contents, I devised several methods before I found one that worked.

Ponderings

The Annotated Table of Contents is a necessary road map and organizational tool for student writers and especially for their readers.

Sample Annotated Table of Contents

I.   Cover Explanation
     I composed my cover explanation by clarifying what the illustrations I have pasted on the cover of my portfolio represent and how I now feel as a writer. This was written on May 16.

II. Personal Essay
     For this selection, I chose a diary entry that I wrote on September 25. The assignment was to describe an unusual or memorable event in my life. Using the day that I passed my driving exam, I recalled the event to the best of my ability.

III. In-Class Essay
     The purpose of this assignment was to show how well students can write in class for a period of ninety minutes on the topic "School lunches." This was completed on November 22.

IV. Literary Analysis
     In my literary analysis, I tried to show how Macbeth, the central character in the play *Macbeth*, is "forced" into the murder of King Duncan. I put a lot of effort into writing this piece and worked through several drafts until I completed the final essay on February 2.

V.   Writer's Selection
     This was a paper that I wrote for my government class. It is a short essay on how I feel about victimless crimes. I think it shows my voice. It was completed on March 25.

VI. Reflection
     My closing letter explains how I progressed as a writer throughout the year and sums up how I felt about each piece in my portfolio. I also talked about my favorite writing assignment in the writer's selection. This letter was completed in early May.

Lesson Plans for Teaching Writing edited by Chris Jennings Dixon © 2007 National Council of Teachers of English.

Figure 2.7

LESSON 25
AUTHENTIC MEASUREMENTS: PORTFOLIO READING PROCEDURES

Chris Jennings Dixon

Purpose

- To provide outside evaluation of student-prepared portfolios as evidence of readiness for college composition

Preparation

This activity motivates alignment of curriculum from high school to college while it also values the composition work high school students complete in their senior year. Preparation for a portfolio presentation requires (1) teacher workshops on portfolio preparation, (2) student development of reflective practices in collecting and revising written work for presentation, (3) faculty training to recognize features of successful portfolio presentations, (4) establishment of criteria for rubrics to be used for assessment of portfolios, (5) development of anchor portfolios as standards for rubrics, and (6) sharing portfolio table of contents and rubrics with students.

Props/Materials

- High School Portfolio (Table of Contents) handout (Figure 2.8)
- Placement Portfolio Scoring Guide handout (Figure 2.9)
- Senior-Year Portfolio Presentation handout (Figure 2.10)
- Portfolio Placement Flowchart handout (Figure 2.11)

Process/Procedure

1. Ongoing professional development workshops and informal discussions are scheduled to assist teachers in portfolio instruction.
2. Students develop yearlong works-in-progress portfolios of their written work using High School Portfolio and Placement Portfolio Scoring Guide handouts as guides to items to select and assess written material for their portfolios.

3. Teachers assist students in reflection, revision, and collection of selected pieces for presentation.

4. Teachers or college personnel present information to students about the opportunity to use high school portfolios as alternative methods of placement in college composition coursework. (See Senior-Year Portfolio Presentation handout.)

5. The process of gathering student portfolios for outside evaluation commences. (See Portfolio Placement Flowchart handout.)

6. High school and college instructors meet to review selected student work to develop and/or refine rubrics for evaluation of portfolios. Using the Placement Portfolio Scoring Guide as a starting point, instructors mutually agree upon traits of successful papers and identify anchor (sample) papers that demonstrate various levels of proficiency.

7. Teachers prepare class lists of students who are interested in submitting their portfolios for outside evaluation.

8. Students prepare final presentation portfolios:

   ▪ Materials should be on one side, printed in ink or word processed, not stapled.

   ▪ No covers or protectors should be used.

   ▪ Only the title page should have student, class, and school identification information. (Inside identifying information should be blacked or whited out.)

9. Students photocopy their portfolios and submit one copy in camera-ready format. (Students may also submit registration materials to the college indicating their interest in attending.)

10. Code numbers are assigned by the college to student portfolios for anonymity in evaluation.

11. Three copies of each portfolio are made for multiple readings.

12. Anchoring session is held to identify range of selected portfolios according to rubrics.

13. Portfolio readers receive six copies of unlabeled anchor portfolios for norming session prior to actual portfolio reading session.

14. Portfolio reading session is held to determine student placements. Each portfolio is read by two readers. If necessary, a third reading may be used for discrepant placements.

15. Results are calculated, reviewed, and verified.

16. Students, teachers, and counselors receive results of portfolio placement readings.

17. Placement letters are sent to students. Placement letters may be used as evidence of placement decisions for a one-year period as students register for college coursework.

Pointers or Pitfalls

Maintaining communication among all participants is essential to this process. The schedule of due dates and sessions needs to be mutually established early in the process to ensure careful planning. Matching college and high school schedules is tricky, and all efforts need to be taken to identify possible conflicts, such as schoolwide testing programs and report card dates. Additionally, having a coordinator from the college to work with all of the participants is vital.

Ponderings

At our site, we used a calendar of due dates that encouraged students to submit portfolios prior to their spring break in order to return placement decisions before high school graduation. Initially, this seemed to parallel "senioritis," a time when many students become restless in the last weeks prior to graduation. However, as the portfolio activity evolved, we found students were very conscientious about their presentations, and many of them wanted more time to produce their final work. Thus, rescheduling submission due dates for the end of senior semester and scheduling placement sessions during the summer should be considered.

High School Portfolio
English 12

Annotated Table of Contents
This should be about one paragraph per annotation/description of each writing assignment.

Opening Piece
      The writer may answer the following:
      Describe student's writing style.
      Describe student's experience with writing.
      Predict how writing may play a role in his or her career choice.

Personal Narrative*

Literary Analysis*

In-Class Essay*

Writer's Selection*

Process Reflective Letter for One Piece*
      The writer may answer the following:
      What steps did the student take to arrive at a first draft?
      What kinds of changes did he or she make from one draft to the next?
      How did teacher/peer conferencing help the student in writing the
         composition?

Closing Reflective Letter for the Portfolio
      The writer may respond to the following:
      Which writing assignment did the student believe to be his or her
         best work and why?
      Which writing assignment did he or she find the most difficult and
         why?
      Which of the student's writing goals does this portfolio illustrate?
      What did the student learn from preparing the portfolio?

*Items identified with an asterisk denote selections that may be used to demonstrate the entire writing process for the Process Reflective Letter.

Lesson Plans for Teaching Writing edited by Chris Jennings Dixon © 2007 National Council of Teachers of English.

Figure 2.8

Placement Portfolio Scoring Guide

4   The texts demonstrate that the writer can successfully complete at least three kinds of writing tasks, and the student's reflective commentary confirms how the work was completed. This is a writer whose composing processes are visible. The texts in the portfolio show that the writer is "coachable": is able to take feedback from peers and teachers and use it appropriately in developing texts. The style and content are sophisticated and mature; the writing demonstrates risk taking in tone and handling of subject matter. Standard Written English is used throughout the texts. The texts are free of surface errors or major grammatical errors that interfere with meaning.

3   The texts demonstrate that the writer can complete some essential writing tasks, though some are completed far better than others. The reflective commentary suggests that the writer's composing processes are still evolving; some process is visible. The writer is still learning how to be "coached." Generally, the writing is proficient but is not sophisticated or mature in style or in attention to audience. (For example, writer adequately handles subject matter but texts demonstrate little evidence of complex or varied sentence patterns; there is little evidence of risk taking in tone or content.) The writing is relatively error-free and demonstrates adequate use of Standard Written English. The texts have minimal surface or grammatical errors that interfere with meaning.

2   The texts demonstrate that the writer can complete one essential writing task and can attempt others. The reflective commentary is emerging and underdeveloped. The writer can talk about the texts but is not willing or able to make essential changes; he or she has not learned to revise. There is little evidence of a composing process. The style and content are unsophisticated and immature. (For example, there is little evidence of varied sentence patterns; writing is not substantial in subject matter.) The texts frequently include errors in Standard Written English that interfere with meaning, e.g., syntactic errors, faulty predication.

1   The texts show an emerging writer. This writer can focus on a task and attempt completion in abbreviated (unelaborated) form but is not fluent and shows no evidence of composing process. Successive drafts are highly redundant (with no significant changes in drafts, no stronger voice, purpose, or attention to audience). The writer is still learning to control written expression. This writer writes very little reflective commentary, and the reflection that is included is oriented to surface features like spelling and capitalization. The writer does not seem to know how to improve writing. Texts demonstrate undeveloped style and simplistic handling of content. Errors in Standard Written English interfere with meaning throughout the texts.

Lesson Plans for Teaching Writing edited by Chris Jennings Dixon © 2007 National Council of Teachers of English.

Figure 2.9

Senior-Year Portfolio Presentation

Who: **YOU** are invited to submit your senior year high school portfolio to determine your readiness for college level work.

What: Your **Portfolio** allows you to demonstrate your best work, creativity, writing, and thinking processes.

Where: Your English class has been selected as a project site to submit portfolios as a substitute for traditional placement methods.

When: Portfolios are due to your English class by _____.

Why: 1. Students who prepare portfolios are more likely to <u>enroll directly</u> in college transfer English classes and avoid expenses of paying for noncredit developmental/remedial courses.

2. Students who are admitted to college with portfolio placements have historically earned <u>higher grades</u> than students admitted with traditional placement tools.

3. Students who are admitted to college with portfolio placement <u>complete</u> their college education more quickly than students admitted with traditional placement tools.

4. You will find that many four-year colleges and universities also have portfolio programs that <u>exempt</u> students from freshman English.

5. You will receive <u>feedback</u> from a reader outside of your English class.

How: Review the **Portfolio Procedures, Table of Contents,** and **Scoring Guide** with your English teacher and submit your **PORTFOLIO!**

Lesson Plans for Teaching Writing edited by Chris Jennings Dixon © 2007 National Council of Teachers of English.

Figure 2.10

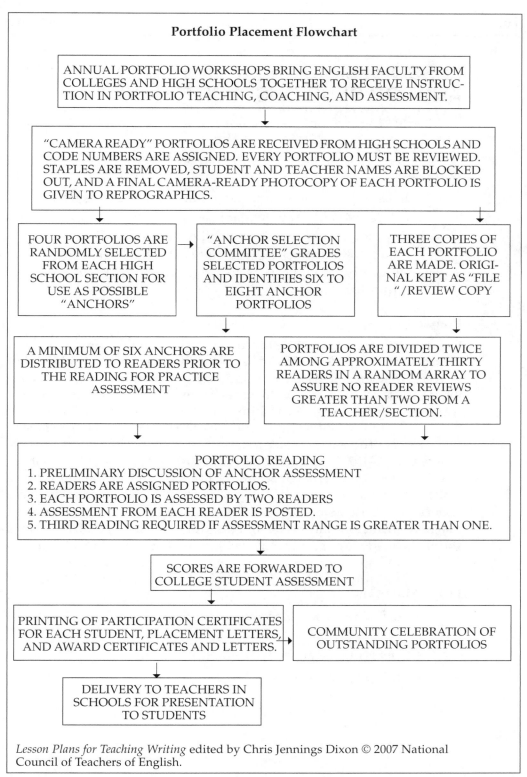

Portfolio Placement Flowchart

ANNUAL PORTFOLIO WORKSHOPS BRING ENGLISH FACULTY FROM COLLEGES AND HIGH SCHOOLS TOGETHER TO RECEIVE INSTRUCTION IN PORTFOLIO TEACHING, COACHING, AND ASSESSMENT.

"CAMERA READY" PORTFOLIOS ARE RECEIVED FROM HIGH SCHOOLS AND CODE NUMBERS ARE ASSIGNED. EVERY PORTFOLIO MUST BE REVIEWED. STAPLES ARE REMOVED, STUDENT AND TEACHER NAMES ARE BLOCKED OUT, AND A FINAL CAMERA-READY PHOTOCOPY OF EACH PORTFOLIO IS GIVEN TO REPROGRAPHICS.

FOUR PORTFOLIOS ARE RANDOMLY SELECTED FROM EACH HIGH SCHOOL SECTION FOR USE AS POSSIBLE "ANCHORS"

"ANCHOR SELECTION COMMITTEE" GRADES SELECTED PORTFOLIOS AND IDENTIFIES SIX TO EIGHT ANCHOR PORTFOLIOS

THREE COPIES OF EACH PORTFOLIO ARE MADE. ORIGINAL KEPT AS "FILE "/REVIEW COPY

A MINIMUM OF SIX ANCHORS ARE DISTRIBUTED TO READERS PRIOR TO THE READING FOR PRACTICE ASSESSMENT

PORTFOLIOS ARE DIVIDED TWICE AMONG APPROXIMATELY THIRTY READERS IN A RANDOM ARRAY TO ASSURE NO READER REVIEWS GREATER THAN TWO FROM A TEACHER/SECTION.

PORTFOLIO READING
1. PRELIMINARY DISCUSSION OF ANCHOR ASSESSMENT
2. READERS ARE ASSIGNED PORTFOLIOS.
3. EACH PORTFOLIO IS ASSESSED BY TWO READERS
4. ASSESSMENT FROM EACH READER IS POSTED.
5. THIRD READING REQUIRED IF ASSESSMENT RANGE IS GREATER THAN ONE.

SCORES ARE FORWARDED TO COLLEGE STUDENT ASSESSMENT

PRINTING OF PARTICIPATION CERTIFICATES FOR EACH STUDENT, PLACEMENT LETTERS, AND AWARD CERTIFICATES AND LETTERS.

COMMUNITY CELEBRATION OF OUTSTANDING PORTFOLIOS

DELIVERY TO TEACHERS IN SCHOOLS FOR PRESENTATION TO STUDENTS

Lesson Plans for Teaching Writing edited by Chris Jennings Dixon © 2007 National Council of Teachers of English.

Figure 2.11

LESSON 26
ANCHOR SESSIONS: PORTFOLIO EVALUATION

Ann Louise Johnston

Purpose

- To assess student writing using outside of the class readers/graders
- To promote inner-reader reliability among diverse portfolio-graders using mutually established portfolio rubrics
- To produce a set of portfolios that can be used to guide future assessments

Preparation

Preliminary steps need to be taken to develop a set of commonly held rubrics for writing. Once rubrics have been designed and refined in pilot settings, they may be used as a standard for subsequent portfolio readings. Rubrics should be reviewed regularly to determine that there is continued agreement and reliability in their application.

A facilitator skilled in portfolio methodology needs to be identified for this process. Using a process of selection that provides a sampling of all portfolios to be read, the facilitator selects a range of portfolios, from ten to fifteen, that seem to run the gamut in student writing skills. Additionally, a team of seven to nine faculty members who have experience in assessment of writing needs to be formed. A common place and time should be designated for the team meeting. Efforts should be made to obtain a comfortable room and provide refreshments for a lengthy session.

Props/Materials

- Portfolio Rubrics/Placement Portfolio Scoring Guide (Figure 2.9, page 73)
- Copies of past anchor portfolios, if available
- Multiple copies of portfolio samples

Process/Procedure

Before the Meeting

1. The facilitator gives the evaluators the portfolio rubrics and copies of selected portfolios to read and evaluate prior to the meeting.
2. Evaluators assign a rubric score to each portfolio

At the Meeting

1. The facilitator reads through the rubrics to be sure evaluators understand the key distinguishing characteristics.
2. Readers are cautioned to adhere to the tenets of each rubric to avoid subjective decisions.
3. The team needs to understand how to evaluate specific situations, such as incomplete assignments, assignments incorrectly followed, or incomplete portfolios.
4. The examination process begins by starting with portfolios that the facilitator has prescreened for possible middle range rubric scores.
5. Readers review portfolios in a sequence as identified by the facilitator.
6. Each reader offers a score and explains his or her rationale by referring to the rubrics.
7. Discussion ensues to reach a consensus and assign a score to each portfolio. If not possible, the most difficult portfolio assessments are identified as items to share at actual portfolio reading sessions.
8. The team proceeds to review portfolios to identify ones that represent the higher and lower ends of the rubric scale.
9. Each portfolio is thoroughly discussed to assign a mutually agreed upon score.
10. If discussion reveals a problem in the rubric, changes in scoring are suggested.
11. Guided by the facilitator, the team identifies outstanding examples of portfolios that represent each score on the rubric scale.

12. Using portfolios that represent all levels of the rubric as well as some that seem to fall between the levels, the team reviews their selections.

13. With consensus agreement of all readers, the facilitator presents the six anchor portfolios to be used for subsequent readings.

Pointers or Pitfalls

Team members may be opinionated and strongly vocal about their views. Be prepared for this. Some graders have personal biases about certain errors, subjects, or styles of writing. To avoid falling into this trap, encourage readers to refer to the rubric. It is not the purpose of the session to arrange portfolios in order from best to worst. Adherence to the rubric to determine a score is the purpose of the session. The facilitator has to be a good manager who enlists the opinions of all participants. No one member should dominate the group or strong-arm decisions. The facilitator should be sure to tell members at the end how valuable their work has been so that they leave with a feeling of accomplishment.

Ponderings

It is hard to distinctively score a portfolio that is strong at one level but may be pushed a bit higher as a weak example of the next rubric level. Finding a perfect "4" or "3" is often difficult as a multitude of factors contribute to the strengths or weaknesses of a portfolio. To maintain a four-point rubric, readers cannot assign half-point values. The tendency to move to the middle can contribute to an averaging of portfolio contents.

LESSON 27
ELECTRONIC PORTFOLIOS WORK FOR ME: DEVELOPING WEBSITES

Bonnie Startt

Purpose

- To investigate the value of writing in present and future careers

- To prepare for writing in a future working environment
that values technology

Preparation

A list of possible local employers needs to be prepared for students to contact. Ideally, students can suggest sites based upon places they have worked or are working.

Props/Materials

Students need access to computers and web hosting sites. There are many free Web hosting sites on the Internet that offer simple to use prepared template Web pages, such as www.free-webhosts.com/. The student does not need to know how to program to create a Web page. Most students find themselves published on the Internet in one class period.

Process/Procedure

Students are instructed to conduct informational interviews of employers to discover the importance of written and verbal communication in getting and keeping a job. Students record and share their findings in small groups and in open discussion with the class.

The employers often relate how competitive the job market has gotten over the last few years. In many cases, students learn that writing skills can provide the difference between layoffs and continued employment, especially in high-tech industries. Individually, students predict how writing may help them as employees to be retained and promoted.

To engage students further in preparing their skills for the job market, I introduce the electronic or digital portfolio to showcase their findings. Students are assigned additional job-related topics and research assignments directed at becoming more familiar with their prospective or existing areas of employment. Using the electronic portfolio mode of posting their writing, projects, research, and findings to their own websites, students share their work and are encouraged to improve their communication skills.

Pointers or Pitfalls

The hope is that over the next few years students will add to their sites. Eventually, each student will have an excellent tool for demonstrating his or her abilities in communication to future employers.

Ponderings

This activity has so many real-life applications that students are truly enthusiastic. They will all be using computers in the real world, so this is just one tool to get them started. Students are enthusiastic about writing because they can see how it will make a difference in their lives. Just as important, they gain technical experience that can be used in future classes as well as on the job. I am constantly amazed at how hard they work to create their Web pages. As they share their websites with each other, they eagerly share their newfound knowledge with their classmates. The learning curve is phenomenal; they do far more than the minimum I require for the class. The electronic portfolio takes on a life of its own in my classes. My students and I have become enthusiastic supporters.

III Literature

"How do I incorporate more writing in my classroom when I am required to 'cover' my curriculum?" is a common concern voiced by teachers who want to ensure that their students are prepared for the rigors of college writing. To develop students' abilities to read and think critically, the following activities embed components of the writing process while also engaging readers in a study of the content of curricular material. Teachers share how they have used literature as a context for writing and thus made the writing process an ongoing focus throughout the year. Through collaboration, a common denominator in many of these strategies, students are encouraged to view literature as a springboard for reflection and analysis. Although some of these activities refer to specific literary works, instructional suggestions can be easily adapted for use with other works and curricula.

LESSON 28
HOT TOPICS: A PREWRITING TECHNIQUE

Julie Herwick

Purpose

- To practice prewriting skills in response to literature-based prompts

Preparation

To prepare students to read Harper Lee's *To Kill a Mockingbird* and consider the issues presented by the author, survey students to promote a discussion of commonly held beliefs, such as "All men are created equal." Ask students to relate personal experiences that demonstrate the truth or falsity of such statements.

Props/Materials

To Kill a Mockingbird by Harper Lee (1960)
Class copies of the following list of statements:

1. All men are created equal.

2. Girls should act like girls.

3. It's okay to be different.

4. Nobody is all bad or good.

5. Some words are so offensive that they should never be stated or written.

6. Under our justice system, all citizens are treated fairly in our courts of law.

7. The old adage, "Sticks and stones may break your bones, but words will never hurt you," is true.

8. Speaking standard grammar proves that a person is smart.

9. A hero is born not made.

10. No one is above the law.

11. Education is the great equalizer.

12. When the law does not succeed in punishing criminals, citizens should do so.

Process/Procedure

Assign students to work in groups with one designated scribe per group. Distribute the list of statements. Ask each group to review each statement and arrive at a consensus as to whether they agree or disagree with the commentary. After group consensus is reached, ask a student speaker from each group to share their findings. From the discussion that ensues, take note of the "hot topics"—those that cause the most controversy. Keep this list of "hot topics" posted and refer to it while discussing the novel.

Pointers or Pitfalls

These "hot topics" provide good starting points for students to develop essays based upon their reading of the novel.

Ponderings

This process may be adapted for use with any novel study to stimulate student interest and engagement in identifying the author's intent.

LESSON 29
FREEWRITING: A PREREADING TECHNIQUE

Charles W. Hoofnagle

Purpose

- To increase comprehension and foster retention

Preparation

The instructor should inform the students that, prior to reading a designated piece of literature—prose (fiction/nonfiction), poetry, drama—they are going to engage in a process that will create more attuned minds and enable them to better understand and comprehend what they are about to read.

Props/Materials

- Reading selection
- Freewriting handout (Figure 3.1)

Process/Procedure

Discuss the following freewriting guidelines before students begin the activity:

1. Write down whatever comes into your mind about the subject of the reading selection before you read it.

2. Don't correct words or cross them out. Just get on paper as many ideas as you can think of, no matter how silly or strange they seem.

3. Strive to keep your pen or pencil moving during the time allocated.

Review and discuss the freewriting sample on the handout. Make sure to give students a specified time period to complete the activity. Next, assign a reading of the selected material. Finally, provide ongoing opportunities for students to review and discuss their freewriting material to determine connections to the reading selection.

Pointers or Pitfalls

Freewriting runs contrary to normal composition endeavors. This point should be stressed to the students; they should not be bothered with violating accepted written composition rules during this process. The instructor should be alert for students who stop writing during the process or who pause to reflect or decide what to write next. It is important to the concept of freewriting that the students write continuously, literally without lifting pen or pencil from paper.

Ponderings

True learning occurs when the unknown (that which is to be learned) is connected to the known (that which has already been learned). The purpose of using freewriting as a prereading technique is to draw students closer to the subject and content of material they are about to read. This connection increases comprehension of the material and fosters a longer lasting retention.

Freewriting: A Prereading Technique

PURPOSE:
To write freely about the subject of the piece or selection that you are going to read so that you are mentally prepared to read the selection.

HOW TO DO IT:

A. Write down whatever comes into your mind about the subject of the reading selection BEFORE you read it.

B. Don't correct words or cross them out. Just get on paper as many ideas as you can think of, no matter how silly or strange they seem.

C. Strive to keep your pen or pencil moving during the predetermined allocated time for the freewriting exercise.

AN EXAMPLE USING THE TOPIC—"ILLEGAL DRUGS":
"Illegal drugs. Drugs that are illegal. What are illegal drugs? Why would someone want to take them? To ruin their bodies? Why do that? A few minutes of pleasure. I don't do drugs. Not because it's wrong. Because it's just not worth it. I have a friend (?) who's always trying to get me to do drugs. He's hooked. He's not a friend at all. And what about the money? They're not free you know! Drugs—drugs—drugstore. Do they call it that anymore? Oh, yeah. That's legal drugs. A girl in my class got sick at a party one time because she took drugs. What kind? What happens when you take them? What happened to her? I bet she felt bad when they wore off. How to stop people. Classes in school? Won't stop people. Some will do it even if peers say don't. Driving and drugging don't mix. Dangerous. Could kill yourself . . . and OTHERS! Wouldn't want to be in their shoes. Don't understand. Just don't understand. Immaturity? Yeah, maybe. Going along with the crowd. Is it worth it? No. Bah!"

Do you see how this student puts down whatever thoughts come into his or her head (without regard to correct grammar or writing form) about the reading selection even before reading it? The student is tapping into his or her own experiences. These written thoughts will provide the basis for connections to the written material, even if some of the thoughts are not even mentioned in the material.

Here are the KEY BENEFITS: When you read a selection, many points in the selection will be familiar to you prior to your reading. You will comprehend new material better and retain the ideas and information for a longer period of time by beginning with a freewriting activity.

Lesson Plans for Teaching Writing edited by Chris Jennings Dixon © 2007 National Council of Teachers of English.

Figure 3.1

LESSON 30
LITERARY TEA PARTY: INFERRING AND PREDICTING

Sherri Bova

Purpose

- To develop prereading skills of inference and prediction
- To reflect on previous inferences or predictions

Preparation

Compose a sheet of words and phrases taken from the story to be read. For instance, in a study of Geoffrey Chaucer's "The Pardoner's Tale," phrases like "Death is dead!" and words like *avarice* can be written on narrow strips of paper. Produce as many strips as there are students in the class, all with different words and phrases printed on them from the literary work.

Props/Materials

Strips with phrases; light refreshments

Process/Procedure

1. For students to practice inferring and predicting the substance of a story by reading and discussing titles of selected works, the teacher identifies a work to be read by the class and prepares excerpts as described.

2. Students are instructed to supply a sheet of notebook paper at the beginning of the activity. They are instructed to come to the refreshment table, take a muffin, a box of juice, and a strip of paper.

3. Once all students have done so, they are instructed to have a tea party and gossip to each other about what is on their strips of paper. They are to move around the room and exchange information, writing each tidbit learned in their notebooks. (Allow them to roam for about twenty minutes and then call them back to order.)

4. Students predict what the story is about based on the information they have gathered during their gossip-fest. The prediction may take the form of a lengthy paragraph, which should be collected, after approximately twenty-five minutes.

5. After the class has read the story, the teacher returns the original paragraphs to students.

6. Students are then instructed to write a reflective paragraph about what they had originally written and compare their earlier responses to their understanding of the actual story. This takes approximately twenty-five minutes.

Pointers or Pitfalls

Students enjoy this activity! Watch the time. When students start discussing the basketball game, it's time to pull them back. The mess on the floor goes without saying.

Ponderings

This activity suggests that the teacher prepare a "tea" for the students, usually consisting of juice and muffins or the like. The goal is to emulate a Gertrude Stein salon with food as a catalyst for group interaction and dialogue. However, if a school ruling forbids bringing food into the classroom, this activity may be conducted without physical sustenance.

LESSON 31
MAKING CONNECTIONS: WRITING AS A REACTION TO READING

Charles W. Hoofnagle

Purpose

- To make connection from author to reader
- To identify writer's purpose

Preparation

Assign the reading of a novel, short story collection, or biography. This activity encourages students to make mental connections with the material during a classroom silent reading period of approximately thirty minutes.

Props/Materials

- Writing as a Reaction to Reading handout (Figure 3.2)
- Reading material (a novel, short story collection, or biography)
- Response journal (spiral notebook)

Process/Procedure

Distribute copies of Writing as a Reaction to Reading handout to provide the necessary background for the writing assignment. Review the handout and the length of the required written reaction (at least a half page). Encourage students to be open and honest regarding their responses.

After the reading session, students record in their journals a "connection" to what they have just read: a feeling, reaction (positive or negative), or sundry thoughts.

An additional option is to budget time for students to discuss their journal entries in pre-assigned teams of four or five or in dyads. This latter activity further strengthens their connections to the reading material by virtue of discussion, allowing students to benefit from the reflections of others.

Pointers or Pitfalls

Students should be constantly reminded that their journal entries are not plot summaries or book reports, i.e., they should devote little space to telling about what they have just read. The goal of the writing exercise is to get students to think and respond intellectually and emotionally to their reading. By thus engaging with the reading content, the student is drawn closer to the writer and the writer's purpose, and an enhanced interest or bond with the written material is formed.

Ponderings

Regarding book choices, the teacher should focus on student interest. Often students come to class having done little reading on their own. Personal interest in a book's content is essential to encourage a reading habit that will eventually lead to the student's becoming a lifelong reader.

Writing as a Reaction to Reading

To process your thoughts and explore your ideas relative to what you have read, try writing about it. Writing about reading is extremely useful. It gives you space to pause, reflect, and ultimately to compose—to express what you really think—and to be creative in the effort. This in turn aids you in making a more personal connection with the components of the story. Increased comprehension, greater retention, and pure enjoyment are the results.

For some, it's occasionally difficult to get started. One of the more effective methods to "get you going" is to simply put pen to paper and start writing. Don't overthink. Just write, write, write, and the thoughts will flow.

Your writing in connection with this handout will be in one of the following two formats:

1. A freestanding exercise to be done in class or for homework, possibly to be discussed with your team members in a cooperative activity, and subsequently collected by the instructor for review.

2. An entry in your Reading Journal (if that approach is part of the course) and, again, at times shared in the helpful, constructive atmosphere of your team. (The Reading Journal, when used, will be collected periodically for instructor review.)

Guidelines:
- Write at least a half a page; don't just complete a statement. (See the example below.)
- State your feelings, thoughts, reactions, and questions about situations, ideas, actions, characters, settings, symbols, plot, theme, and any other elements of the book.
- You can't be wrong in your responses, so take some risks and be honest.
- Write about what you like or dislike, what seems confusing or unusual to you. Tell what you think something means.
- Make predictions about what might happen later.
- Relate your personal experiences that connect with the plot, characters, or setting.
- Don't just summarize the plot. Let your voice be heard.

> Example: The character Hott Aire in the novel *When the Wild Wind Blows* by Summer Storm reminds me of myself because whenever she gets into trouble, she makes excuses for herself. I tend to do this a lot. Just like Hott when she failed to report Kool Breeze's thieving ways to the authorities because she was focusing on getting her homework done, I have on occasion tried to cover up my mistakes by diverting attention elsewhere. I'll say this: I don't like myself when I behave like Hott did.

Lesson Plans for Teaching Writing edited by Chris Jennings Dixon © 2007 National Council of Teachers of English.

Figure 3.2

LESSON 32
"YOU BE THE JUDGE": CRITICAL RESPONSES TO LITERATURE

Susan B. Slavicz

Purpose

- To develop skill in reading critically and closely
- To participate in oral interpretation of dialogue
- To develop ability to respond to literature in writing

Preparation

Research background on trials and women's place in nineteenth-century Europe.

Props/Materials

A Doll's House by Henrik Ibsen, often anthologized

Process/Procedure

1. Following a reading of *A Doll's House*, students write a paragraph stating their support of Nora or Thorvald's actions.

2. Teacher leads a class on the role of women in Ibsen's society.

3. Students are assigned roles for a trial in which they decide if Nora should be granted a divorce. (Try to give everyone a part—the teams can be large.) Those roles include
    - A judge
    - A jury
    - A foreman
    - People to play each character (including the nurse and housekeeper)
    - A defense lawyer (and team)
    - A prosecuting attorney (and team)

4. Provide time for students (about an hour) to look through the play and decide on their approach. The defense and prosecution can interview the characters and discuss their strategies. The judge and foreman should decide on time limits and the rules of the court.

5. Hold the trial. The students playing characters should only give statements that have support in the text of the play.

6. Ask students to reread the paragraphs they wrote after they read the play.

7. Assign an additional paragraph for students to either agree or disagree with their first opinions and support those opinions with information from the play and the trial.

Pointers or Pitfalls

Students do need time to prepare for the trial. The instructor needs to set a time limit for the trial—and then allow the judge and foreman to decide how that time will be spent. The jury can be a problem; they should spend the time going over the play together. From the beginning, students need to understand that they must use support from the play for the trial. Students often have trouble understanding the society in which Ibsen's play takes place. A close study of the play forces them to interpret each character's dialogue.

Ponderings

This seems to be a nonintimidating exercise that encourages students to speak in a relaxed setting. It may be easily adapted for other works with controversial outcomes, such as other often anthologized work as Arthur Miller's *Death of a Salesman*, Nathaniel Hawthorne's *The Scarlet Letter*, or Harper Lee's *To Kill a Mockingbird*.

LESSON 33
CHAUCER RAFTS: WRITING A PARODY

Elizabeth H. Beagle

Purpose

- To employ rhetorical devices of role, audience, format, topic, and strong verbs in writing a parody

Preparation

Review the definition of *parody* with the class: "a humorous imitation of a serious piece of literature" and solicit examples from students' exposure to television and movies.

Props/Materials

- Chaucer RAFTS handout (Figure 3.3)
- "The Prologue" from Chaucer's *The Canterbury Tales*, often anthologized

Process/Procedure

1. The teacher assigns students to read "The Prologue" of *The Canterbury Tales*. Conduct a class discussion on the prologue and the stereotypes presented. Broaden the discussion by commenting on various stereotypical people in today's society. Encourage students to make comparisons between Chaucer's time period and today.

2. The teacher distributes the RAFTS handout and leads a class discussion about rhetorical devices contained in the acronym *RAFTS* (role, audience, format, topic, strong verb).

3. Students are asked to identify the RAFTS in the prompt on the Chaucer RAFTS handout and then to write three-paragraph essays using the prompt.

4. The teacher asks students to read their drafts aloud to the class.

5. The students are assigned to work in groups of three to four to participate in peer reviews of their drafts.

6. The teacher asks students to identify and copy the RAFTS from the other student papers in their groups.

7. The teacher assigns each group to write an introduction and a conclusion for their collected group "prologue."

Pointers or Pitfalls

The *RAFTS* acronym (role, audience, format, topic, strong verb) was coined by Nancy Vandeventer of Bozeman Jr. High School, Bozeman, Montana, for the 1978 Montana Writing Program. The approach can be used to develop a prompt for writing or to respond to a prompt. Be sure to review each rhetorical element by illustrating its use with examples.

Ponderings

This is a great way to show students that our world has not changed greatly from that of Chaucer's. It is also a good activity to promote teamwork. As with all teamwork, the teacher must ensure that all students contribute to the writing process.

Chaucer RAFTS*

YOU are Geoffrey Chaucer writing to a twentieth-first-century audience. You are going on a memorial pilgrimage to the site of the 2001 destruction of the World Trade Center in New York City. You have just begun working on your masterpiece, *The Canterbury Tales*, when you meet the other pilgrims. You decide to wile away the time by writing a description of the various types of people on the pilgrimage. You decide to include one-paragraph descriptions of their clothing, their possessions, their companions, their sins, vices, and virtues, their physical characteristics, their personality traits, and their apparent motivations for the pilgrimage.

Directions
Create a three-paragraph essay using RAFTS in which you describe the characteristics and actions of one of the modern-day pilgrims on his or her way to New York City.

*RAFTS is an acronym for a rhetorical situation for writing that includes
 Role of the writer
 Audience
 Format of the writing
 Topic of discussion
 Use of a **S**trong verb

Lesson Plans for Teaching Writing edited by Chris Jennings Dixon © 2007 National Council of Teachers of English.

Figure 3.3

LESSON 34
"TRASHY POETRY": IMPROVING WORD CHOICE

Mary F. Rezac

Purpose

- To improve word choice in writing

Preparation

Identifying items and preparing an inventory of items in the wastebasket or trash can located in the classroom can be an anticipatory phase of this activity.

Props/Materials

- Copy of Shel Silverstein's poem "Sarah Cynthia Sylvia Stout," in *Where the Sidewalk Ends*
- Garbage can (full of clean, teacher-selected items)
- Construction paper

Process/Procedure

1. Tell students that "Today, we are going to talk trash!" First, model the assignment using the classroom wastebasket or trash can.

2. Then assign the students the task of taking an inventory of their trash or garbage can at home. Instruct them to write down a description of each item that includes at least one adjective.

3. The next day in class, read aloud the poem entitled "Sarah Cynthia Sylvia Stout" by Shel Silverstein. Discuss word choice and the selection of powerful and "juicy" adjectives that create pictures in the reader's mind.

4. Instruct students to return to their own lists with descriptions of items in their trash and create their own poems. (They can design their own form or follow the format of Shel Silverstein's.)

5. For presentation, ask students to draw a large trash can as the background of their final drafts.

Pointers or Pitfalls

Make sure students have at least ten to fifteen items of trash to work with when creating their poems. It might take them more than one day to do this.

Ponderings

Kids really get into describing their trash. They love hearing from other students what is in different people's garbage! This activity is an opportunity for students to talk "trash" without getting into trouble.

LESSON 35
AN AFFECTION FOR ALLITERATION: USING SOUND EFFECTS

Mary Virginia Allen

Purpose

- To employ sound effects in writing
- To analyze the use and effects of alliteration

Preparation

The teacher should prepare handouts similar to the sample provided and review the use of alliteration in literature and the media with the class prior to distributing the handouts.

Props/Materials

- Dictionaries
- An Affection for Alliteration handout (Figure 3.4)

Process/Procedure:

1. Students review the definition of *alliteration*, read samples provided by the teacher, and consider the writer's purpose in using sound effects.

2. The teacher gives An Appreciation for Alliteration handout to each student.

3. After distributing the handouts, the teacher guides the class in a discussion of alliteration and its uses. (Approximately ten minutes should be given for students to complete this exercise.)

4. Students complete the tasks on the handout.

5. The teacher provides time for students to share their creative results orally.

Pointers or Pitfalls

Decide beforehand if students are allowed to add alliterative words to the list to create their word groups.

Ponderings

This can be a good transition exercise from writing with alliterative phrases to studying the use of alliteration in reading and analyzing poetry.

An Affection for Alliteration

Just what is ***alliteration?*** Read the following sentence and see if you can determine a definition:

As Jane joined her jubilant friends, the judge jumped into his jersey suit and jogged joyously to his judo lesson.

Alliteration is _____.

Alliteration is a device used in both prose and poetry to achieve a variety of effects. What effect did the alliteration have in the silly sentence above?
What effect does alliteration have in the following sentence?

The raging river rolled rumbling over the rocks.

Share your ideas with classmates.

Exercise: Look at the following list of words and select groups of three that begin with the same consonant sound. Think about the effect that you want to create, as in sound effect or mood effect. Be sure that all three words in each group have some sort of relationship so that your groups "make sense." Humor is definitely acceptable. Remember that sometimes words begin with unlike letters but have the same beginning sound. The *sound* of the letter beginning each word is the clue. Write your combinations on the lines provided. Remember, if you don't know the meaning of a word, refer to a dictionary!

wobbly   brook   weak red   ruffled   crisp   gift   plain   sticky   plush
wicked   man   toy   rancid   gala   radish   cat   dog   black   broken
wavering   ghoulish   car   gray   bleak   staunch   baby   blanched   rowdy
wrecked   gilded   curly   round   wild   rose   gruff   precious   celery   silvery
damp   magical   wonderful   box   green   waffle   grouchy   ball   girl   wide
brass   musical   monstrous   boy   snake   runt   blue   kale   golden   slithering
blustery   grand   bouncing   cloud   crate   gross   lake   bread   mind   branch

_____

_____

_____

_____

_____

_____

Figure 3.4

LESSON 36
"GOOD NIGHT SAIGON": FIGURES OF SPEECH IN LYRICS

Susan P. Allen

Purpose

- To identify figurative language that conveys effective imagery

Preparation

Define and give examples of similes, metaphors, and puns.

Props/Materials

- Lyrics to Billy Joel's "Goodnight Saigon" available at http://lyrics.rare-lyrics.com/B/Billy-Joel/Goodnight-Saigon.html
- Recording of Billy Joel's "Goodnight Saigon" (tape or CD)
- Equipment to play recording (cassette player or computer with CD drive)

Process/Procedure

1. Provide access for students to song lyrics of "Goodnight Saigon" and direct them to print all stanzas.
2. Ask students to identify similes, metaphors, and puns or word plays in the lyrics as they listen to a recording of "Goodnight Saigon."
3. Ask students, sitting in groups of three to four, to compare what they identified with the findings of their group members.
4. Assign a response piece for students to comment on the impact of the imagery.
5. Review song lyrics as a class to confirm identification of similes, metaphors, and puns in the work.

Pointers or Pitfalls

This activity should be a follow-up to a study of imagery. Color coding the responses may help students to delineate separate elements of figurative language. Musically inclined students should be encouraged to play the melody and/or sing the lyrics.

Ponderings

Students enjoy the musical aspect of this activity. Additional selections may be included. If students are asked to bring in their favorite songs, they should be warned that any lyrics that are in poor taste will not be acceptable for classroom study.

LESSON 37
"WHAT'S IN A NAME?" DECODING CHARACTERIZATION

Sue Buck

Purpose

- To identify elements of characterization
- To make interpersonal connections with literature

Preparation

To generate thought and discussion about each student's name as a stepping stone to Sandra Cisneros's book *The House on Mango Street*, instruct students to read the chapter entitled "My Name" in which the main character discusses her name, "Esperanza."

Props/Materials

- What's in a Name? handout (Figure 3.5)
- Two student samples (Figure 3.6)

Process/Procedure

1. Distribute the handout What's in a Name? to provide suggestions for discussion and writing.
2. Review student samples.
3. Allow time for students to respond to the prompts.

4. In small groups, ask students to compare their paragraphs and select sample paragraphs that discuss some, many, or all of the questions proposed. (Ten to fifteen minutes)

5. Solicit volunteers to read their paragraphs aloud to the class.

Pointers or Pitfalls

This is very personal writing, so encourage students to share their thoughts aloud in class discussion. After students realize how others have been named, the more reluctant students will also join in. Student samples may also be used to motivate students to respond to the prompt.

What's in a Name?

1. What is your full given name?

2. What is the history, origin, or definition of your name?

3. How and why did your parents choose the name they gave you?

4. What nicknames have you had?

5. What attitudes do people display toward your name?

6. What influence has your name had on your life—advantages or disadvantages?

7. Would you prefer another name? If so, what and why?

Lesson Plans for Teaching Writing edited by Chris Jennings Dixon © 2007 National Council of Teachers of English.

Figure 3.5

"What's in a Name?"—Student Samples

My full name is Kristen Eva Brown. I hate it. I asked my parent why they gave it to me, and they said *Kristen* is because they couldn't compromise on Krista or Eva Marie, so they just somehow came up with Kristen Eva. *Eva* was my great grandma's name on my dad's side, and then later we found out that her name wasn't Eva but Evee. And then *Brown* because, unfortunately, that was my dad's last name. Oh, yeah, my dad hated the name Krista Eva because he thought it sounded to much like Christmas Eve. How retarded!

Ruben Rios: The reason I got my name is because my grandfather's name was Ruben and he passed it to my dad and then my dad passed it to me. I don't think that I am gonna do the same. The way I got my last name was somewhere a long time ago my great, great, great grandfather liked to be in the water and go camping by rivers and fish and that kind of stuff, so he changed his last name to "Rios" which means "Rivers" and it has been that for many years now. I would not want another name because you don't hear my name often unless you are around a lot of Mexicans.

Lesson Plans for Teaching Writing edited by Chris Jennings Dixon © 2007 National Council of Teachers of English.

Figure 3.6

LESSON 38
"FIBBLESTAX AND CARR":
UNDERSTANDING CHARACTERIZATION

James Blasingame Jr.

Purpose

- To improve process and word choice in writing
- To develop skill in identifying character traits

Preparation

Previous class time on elements of story/novel (plot, characterization, etc.)

Props/Materials

Fibblestax by Devin Scillian (Kathryn Darnell, illustrator)

Process/Procedure

1. After reading the story of Fibblestax, the nice young man who competed with the evil old man named Carr for the position of namer/word creator, the teacher writes on the board as students brainstorm character traits of the two characters based on (1) the author's description, (2) actions of the two characters, (3) their own dialogue, or (4) the actions and dialogue of other characters about them.

2. Students are then given an index card on which they write "protagonist" on one side and "antagonist" on the other side. Students are asked to make up a name for a protagonist and write it on that side of the card and make up an antagonist to go on the other side. The teacher places all names in a fishbowl and then draws the name for a protagonist and for an antagonist.

3. Placing the names on the board, the teacher asks students as a class to come up with character traits for each character, attempting specific, powerful word choice, and using the four characterization techniques previously mentioned.

4. When substantial lists of character traits are created, the teacher then asks the students to brainstorm possible conflicts between the two characters.

5. Students are directed to write a short story in which they may use the two names, any portion of the brainstorming on characterization, and any of the conflict possibilities from the board. They may also make up their own.

Pointers or Pitfalls

Students come up with an amazingly large number of character traits, and once the characterization begins to get a little silly, it's time to move on. A few students tend to return to inappropriate storylines any time they are given freedom to choose, so outline appropriate story content and insist that students who tend to write about the same thing try something different this time.

Ponderings

The potential richness of characterization springs out of this activity and shows up in students' writing. Don't be surprised if they go a little overboard on their character development for a while; it will even out eventually. This activity also gets them searching for just the right word and might even be facilitated with a thesaurus.

LESSON 39
THE CANTERBURY RAP: MAKING CONNECTIONS THROUGH MEMORIZATION

Dorothy K. Fletcher

Purpose

- To identify connections between ancient and modern use of language

Preparation

Obtain a good recording or reading of the Middle English version of *The Canterbury Tales* so students can get the appropriate cadence. Preview samples of recordings of rap to provide an example of rap rhythm without words.

Props/Materials

- "The Prologue" to Geoffrey Chaucer's *The Canterbury Tales*, often anthologized (Middle English version preferred)
- Samples of rap music

Process/Procedure

1. Students read "The Prologue" and listen to an oral recording of the text.
2. The teacher presents examples of rap rhythm for students to compare and contrast to "The Prologue."
3. Students are assigned memorization and recital of the first eighteen lines of "The Prologue" by a due date.
4. On the performance date, students orally recite the lines in class from memory.

Note: Students have the option of "rapping" the lines and providing musical background for their presentations.

Pointers or Pitfalls

Because the assignment is to memorize "The Prologue," many students are most resistant, at first. However, some of my more musically inclined students take off with this activity and help to bring the others along. Using a rap rhythm helps many of my students see that the older works have as powerful a beat as any work of modern day artists. Additionally, some students are so afraid of public address that they initially refuse to do the assignment. I allow these students to find me prior to the performance day to practice reciting their assignments privately. This pre-session seems to help them gain confidence. Once the deadline has passed; however, all students are required to perform in front of the class.

Ponderings

Bloom's Taxonomy is very clear that memorizing is the least difficult of the levels of learning, so there is no reason why this activity cannot or should not be done. The "rite-of-passage" quality of this assignment is quite gratifying. The connection to rap music is also very exciting, and the audience participation when a young person performs his or her piece with a modern rap musical piece playing in the background is very uplifting for all students in the room.

LESSON 40
"MY HOMETOWN TALES": USING MODELS FOR WRITING

Julie Herwick

Purpose

- To imitate the writing style of an accomplished author in order to develop a greater understanding of the work and the writer
- To adapt time and setting in order to write from a classic model

Preparation

- A close reading of several of Geoffrey Chaucer's *The Canterbury Tales*, often anthologized
- Explanation of "frame" story and the "types" of tales, including the Breton Lai and the Fabliaux

Props/Materials

- A paperback copy of Geoffrey Chaucer's *The Canterbury Tales*, or if not, the anthologized textbook version
- Any film available to give background information on the time period (thirteenth to fourteenth century)
- A list of the seven deadly sins: pride, envy, gluttony, lust, anger, greed, and sloth
- My Hometown Tales handout (Figure 3.7)

Process/Procedure

1. Students are assigned topics of research to discover characteristics of Chaucer's time period.
2. The teacher may present a film depicting the thirteenth to fourteenth centuries for students to identify the elements of setting in Chaucer's tales.
3. Teacher leads students in a discussion of the seven deadly sins and guides students to brainstorm contemporary examples of each sin.

4. Based upon the brainstorm activity, students are assigned present time-related topics to investigate and report on prior to reading *The Canterbury Tales*.

5. Teacher presents an oral reading for the class of a selected tale.

6. Students are assigned to read teacher-selected excerpts from *The Canterbury Tales*.

7. Teacher distributes My Hometown Tales handout.

8. Students write their modern-day imitations of *The Canterbury Tales* in groups.

9. Students read their parodies aloud to the class.

Pointers or Pitfalls

Some of the tales in *The Canterbury Tales* are R-rated, so reading them or having students read them aloud is at the teacher's discretion.

Ponderings

This lesson can be named for the specific town, city, or area of the country where the students live. Working with this activity may reinforce the notion of the universality of sin and promote writing assignments related to this theme.

My Hometown Tales

Assignment

In his prologue, Chaucer presents a realistic portrait of those around him in fourteenth-century England. Choose three pilgrims who may have lived in your town or city. Create a complete story including a prologue and three moral tales defining your characters as you parody Chaucer's style and interpretation of the seven deadly sins today.

Prewriting

Create your characters by choosing characteristics within the categories of social class, personality, and physical appearance. Once you have made these choices, begin your tale by prewriting a prologue containing a brief description of all three characters, plus the reason for their telling of a tale. Then sketch out your story in rough draft form.

Writing

Using the following example as a guide, produce your draft of "My Home-town Tales." Chaucer used couplets in creating his masterpiece. In these couplets, he also used direct characterizations ("This same gentle woman with style and grace") and indirect ones ("Wore ink spotted, chalky dresses of lace") to reflect impoverished conditions.

Example

There was a teacher, a scholarly maid,
In all of the lands, she was poorly paid,
And from the day on which she first started,
Taught lessons in which ignorance departed,
This same gentle woman with style and grace,
Wore ink spotted, chalky dresses of lace.

Grade (100 Points)

Include a prologue for three characters with three tales = 75 points

Dynamic story, vivid verbs, written in couplets of typically eight to ten syllables per line = 25 points

Lesson Plans for Teaching Writing edited by Chris Jennings Dixon © 2007 National Council of Teachers of English.

Figure 3.7

LESSON 41
OBJECTIVE V. SUBJECTIVE: WRITING A SUMMARY

Joseph H. Lemrow

Purpose

- To write a summary from an objective point of view
- To write a summary from a subjective point of view

Preparation

Begin by assigning readings of selected texts. Ask students to decide which readings speak most directly to them.

Props/Materials

Suggested readings, often anthologized:

- Patricia Grace's "Butterflies" (one-page piece of flash fiction)
- Wendy Wasserstein's "The Man in a Case" (one-act play)
- Langston Hughes's "Theme for English B" (poem)
- B. White's "Education" (personal essay)

Note: This activity may be adapted to other works.

Process/Procedure

Students are assigned to write two lengthy paragraphs (six to ten sentences each) that respond to the following student directions:

Paragraph One—Objective Summary

1. Identify the main idea or thesis of the work and write that thought in a sentence of your own wording.

2. Next, determine if the author provided any reasons or explanations for the main idea of his or her work. Again, try to write out those reasons in your own words.

3. Then, identify any clear examples or illustrations the author provided to support his or her claims. Use those examples or illustrations to support your summary of the writer's main ideas.

Paragraph Two—Subjective Summary

1. Identify what arrested your attention and explain why you thought it fascinating. Do not merely tell the reader you found the subject "interesting"; instead, explain what the piece offered that made it relevant to you. Try to determine who you are as a reader; that is, if you are female, do you respond differently to Wasserstein's play than a male reader might? Explain why. Or, if you see Hughes' poem as the product of one seeking access to traditional centers of power (learning, the majority culture), explain whether you believe the author was successful.

2. If you find the material uninspiring, explain why.

3. Remember to refer to specific items in the poem, play, short story, or essay that you believe triggered your individual response. Use those references in your paragraph to support your views.

Pointers or Pitfalls

Remind students to incorporate quotations from the material under analysis. The list of literary works may be altered to include selections that better fit curricular needs. The same approaches to objective and subjective writing can be used.

Ponderings

Emphasizing the objective nature of the first paragraph narrows the student's focus while the subjective nature of the second paragraph lends itself to a freer rein for the student to share his or her impressions. The aims of this task are multiple. As the first writing task in this course, I am anxious to get a read on the general skill level of the class. In addition, I like to encourage students to get in the habit of reading selections from the text in such a way that they identify exactly what the author intends to transmit to the reader.

LESSON 42
MULTIPLE INTELLIGENCES: IDENTIFYING AND USING LEARNING STYLES

Chris Jennings Dixon

Purpose

- To identify and recognize learning styles to nurture thinking and writing

Preparation

Based on Howard Gardner's theory of multiple intelligences in *Frames of Mind*, we know that students have tendencies to solve problems using distinct learning styles. Encouraging students to identify and recognize their learning styles can promote improvements in thinking. Using props on a table representing different approaches to learning, discuss the concept of how each person constructs meaning in response to varied stimuli, such as visually with photographs, verbally with books, musically with recordings, or kinesthetically with paint or clay.

Props/Materials

Resources

- www.mitest.com/o2ndary.htm

  "7 Intelligences Checklist"

- www.literacyworks.org/mi/assessment/findyour strengths.html

  "Assessment: Find Your Strengths"

- www.surfaquarium.com/MI/inventory.htm

  "Multiple Intelligence Inventory"

Sample Projects

- A Hodgepodge of Ideas handout (Figure 3.8)
- *The Stranger* Project handout (Figure 3.9)
- Novel Project: *Brave New World* handout (Figure 3.10)
- Bio-Poem handout (Figure 3.11)
- Shakepearean Plays: *Othello* Project/*Hamlet* Responses handout (Figure 3.12)

Process/Procedure

Students survey and identify their types of intelligence, using one of the suggested websites. After students determine the mental learning styles with which they are most comfortable, remind them that most people are strong in only a few types of intelligences. Adapt or use the Sample Projects to provide alternative approaches to classroom activities. As a follow-up to reading a work of literature, ask students to select an approach to completing a project individually or collaboratively that best demonstrates their learning style.

Pointers or Pitfalls

Many of the project ideas can be adapted to individual curriculum. Students should be encouraged to develop more than one approach to multiple intelligences. You may, however, relate that Albert Einstein used all of his intelligences to solve a problem. Varying instructional approaches provides a nurturing climate for all students. Grading multiple intelligence projects requires establishing introductory rubrics or requirements with the students. Because many of the projects are to be presented to the class, students should be involved in developing criteria and evaluating other students' work.

Ponderings

The majority of students surveyed in our schools were identified as "music smart." This, of course, is no surprise given that the favorite pastime of many students is listening to music. Internet sites such as http://www.rockhall.com/programs/institute.asp, The Rock and Roll Hall of Fame, may be accessed for further instructional activities related to musical/rhythmic intelligence.

A Hodgepodge of Ideas Using Multiple Intelligences

After you have read the assigned novel, select one of the following approaches to completing your project. Be prepared to hand in your materials and to present your project to the class:

1. "That's Entertainment"—Compile a collection of ten songs that a character in your novel would choose as his favorites based upon plot, theme, and character analysis. Create a tape using the music and rhythms of those pieces.

2. "Now A Word from Our Sponsor"—Use a well-known advertisement's refrain to demonstrate the actions and personality of one character in your novel. Present the commercial in costume. Example: McDonald's "I'm Lovin' It" sung by Romeo.

3. "Unfolding Character"—Use a graphic organizer, such as mapping, to depict the relationships between characters in the novel.

4. "News from the Front"—Using themes and situations related to the novel, research the facts of the time period. Then create a more detailed, factually-based characterization of a main character using that information.

5. "You Know What I'm Saying"—Using dialogue from the novel, update the language to convey meaning for contemporary audiences.

6. "You Were There"—Imagine that you are a character in the novel. Write a scene including components of the book with you as a part of the setting and plot.

7. "A Space Odyssey"—Create a timeline for the actions and plot of the novel.

8. "In the Eye of the Beholder" —Draw or sketch or paint five significant scenes from the novel. Include captions for each scene.

9. "What's On?"—Find five media articles that connect to the novel's theme. Place them on a poster with an accompanying paragraph explaining the connection of each article.

10. "Do Not Pass 'GO'"—Create a board game using characters, plot, conflict, theme, and setting of the novel.

Lesson Plans for Teaching Writing edited by Chris Jennings Dixon © 2007 National Council of Teachers of English.

Figure 3.8

The Stranger Project

After reading and discussing *The Stranger* by Albert Camus, you need to decide on one of the following projects to complete and present to the class. You may work individually, in pairs, or in triads. Note the due date for your presentation.

Due Date: _____

1. Draw/Sketch/Create six significant scenes from the novel. Each visual should include an effective caption. Both will be submitted.

2. This novel presents more questions than answers. Write a chapter or scene to insert into *The Stranger*. It must be thoughtful and must model Camus' style. Use this scene to heighten events, characters, themes, or to provide closure. Submit your writing after presenting.

3. The media is filled with current events that focus on the absurdities in life. Cut out five articles that illustrate meaningful purpose to life and five articles that underscore meaninglessness to existence. Write a paragraph connecting the article to Camus' philosophy explored in *The Stranger*. Submit both the articles and paragraphs.

4. Read the song lyrics to "Killing an Arab" by The Cure, which is based on *The Stranger*. Write your own song based on the novel's plot, characters, or theme. You may create your own musical accompaniment or use tape/CD from an artist supplying your original lyrics. Be prepared to submit the lyrics and to present your song.

5. Act out a significant scene from the novel. Rewrite the narrative scene into a dramatic one. Include a title, character list, stage directions, and props. Submit your minidrama after you perform.

6. Review events surrounding Camus' existential outlook on life. Write a myth or tale that demonstrates your philosophy of life. Remember, the audience should be able to clearly identify this philosophy after you present a reading of your myth/tale. Submit the titled writing.

Lesson Plans for Teaching Writing edited by Chris Jennings Dixon © 2007 National Council of Teachers of English.

Figure 3.9

Novel Project: *Brave New World* **by Aldous Huxley**

Decide on one of the following projects to complete individually, in pairs, or in triads:

1. Act out a significant scene from the novel. Rewrite the narrative scene into a dramatic one. As you script it, be sure to include a title, character list, and stage directions. Also, think about staging, props, and effective characterization. You will submit the writing when you perform the scene.

2. Write a song lyric that would demonstrate Huxley's plot/conflict/theme in *Brave New World.* Present this to your own music or borrow a familiar tune providing your original lyrics. You will submit the written lyrics when you perform.

3. The media is filled with current events that focus on technological advancements. Select five current medial issues to cut out and summarize that link the world of today with that of *Brave New World.* Make sure your issues share Huxley's warning about advancement of science without morals or a concern for humanity, and provide parallels for the class when you make your presentation.

4. Draw/Sketch/Create ten visuals of significant scenes from the novel. Each visual should include an effective caption. Both will be submitted.

5. Write a monologue to provide a voice for one of the characters we do not hear in Huxley's text; make sure it provides insight into your chosen character.

6. Draw an illustrated map tracing the action of the plot. Add descriptive labels for each illustration.

7. Rewrite one section/chapter of the novel shifting points of view by writing from the perspective of a minor character. Pay attention to details and remain true to all characters' traits and values.

8. Write a letter to the author, *Dear Mr. Huxley,* in which you critique the novel and share what you like/dislike and any other effective commentary. You may also inform Mr. Huxley about the changes in society from his writing to now.

9. Become a casting director for a movie based upon the novel. Select actors appropriate for each character's role and write a brief statement for each selection that highlights your casting choice.

10. Write a letter exchange from one character in the novel to another that could have been written at a particular time. These should be in appropriate format and may range from a "Dear John" letter to hate mail message.

Lesson Plans for Teaching Writing edited by Chris Jennings Dixon © 2007 National Council of Teachers of English.

Figure 3.10

Bio-Poem

Fill in the appropriate response using one character from the novel you have read. A sample is given from John Steinbeck's *The Grapes of Wrath*.

Line 1 First name	Noah
Line 2 Four words that describe this character	Tall, strange, calm, puzzled
Line 3 Brother/Sister/Son/Daughter of	Brother of Tommy
Line 4 Lover of (three ideas or people)	Lover of peace, isolation, silence
Line 5 Who feels (three ideas)	Who feels laid-back, numb, nothing?
Line 6 Who needs (three ideas)	Who needs a sense of direction, a place in society, pride?
Line 7 Who gives (three ideas)	Who gives peace, amazement, a wondering look?
Line 8 Who fears (three ideas)	Who fears life, other people, himself?
Line 9 Who would like to see (three ideas)	Who would like to see feelings, caring, temptation?
Line 10 Resident of	Resident of Oklahoma
Line 11 Last name	Joad

Monologue:

Select one of the following quotations to use as a fitting epigraph for one character from the novel. Then, stay in character and compose a monologue that connects the message of the quotation to the character:

1. Life's nonsense pierces us with strange relation. (Wallace Stevens)
2. I am the place in which something has occurred. (Claude Lévi-Strauss)
3. Life can only be understood backwards, but it must be lived forwards. (Søren Kierkegaard)
4. We only see what we look at. To look is an act of choice. (John Berger)
5. Quickly got, quickly lost. (Yiddish proverb)
6. Knowledge is the source of all mystery. (Shen-hui)
7. Regret is an appalling waste of energy; you can't build on it; it's only good for wallowing in. (Katherine Mansfield)
8. Too much sunshine makes a desert. (Arabian proverb)
9. When a finger points at the moon, an imbecile looks at the finger. (Chin)

Lesson Plans for Teaching Writing edited by Chris Jennings Dixon © 2007 National Council of Teachers of English.

Figure 3.11

Shakespearean Plays

Othello **Project**

Decide on one of the following projects to complete individually, in pairs, or in triads:

1. Act out a dramatic scene from the original play that has significance. Then modernize the same scene creating a current environment/application. Set this new scene, script it, and provide a dramatic parallel by acting it out.

2. Write a monologue to provide a voice for one of the characters who we do not get to hear in Shakespeare's text. Preface your rendition by letting us know where this soliloquy would fit in the play. Make sure it provides insight into your chosen character.

3. Write a song lyric that would demonstrate Shakespeare's plot/conflict/theme in *Othello*. Present this to your own music or borrow a composed piece providing your original lyrics.

4. Select five current media issues to summarize that link today's world with Shakespeare's through his text, *Othello*. Make sure your issues connect to the play (a passion killing, a daughter betraying her father, a vendetta...), and provide the parallel for the class when you present your project.

5. Create a children's book based on *Othello*. Make sure you adapt the plot to an elementary-level audience. Create illustrations that follow your changed plot line. Package this together to present a reading to the class.

Hamlet **Responses**

Individually, in pairs or triads, apply your insights from reading Shakespeare's *Hamlet* to the following:

Theme Song: Select an appropriate theme song for each of these characters: Hamlet, the Ghost, Claudius, Gertrude, and Rosencrantz and Guildenstern.

One Word: Decide on one word that serves as the most important word for the play so far. Support your selection.

3-2-1: (1) Identify three types of betrayal Hamlet has met. (2) List two courses of action Hamlet must take. (3) Identify the essential conflict Hamlet must face.

You Name It: Select one theme for this play. Using the theme, create a more appropriate title for this tragedy than *Hamlet*.

Parallel Worlds: Focusing on relationships, crimes, and betrayals, select three events from the media today that parallel three events that existed in Hamlet's world.

Lesson Plans for Teaching Writing edited by Chris Jennings Dixon © 2007 National Council of Teachers of English.

Figure 3.12

LESSON 43
ONLINE *HAMLET* DISCUSSION:
ENHANCING CRITICAL THINKING

Susan B. Slavicz

Purpose

- To increase understanding of characterization in the play *Hamlet* by Shakespeare, often anthologized
- To develop critical thinking ability

Preparation

Develop questions that require students to interpret the actions of the play.

Props/Materials

- Access to computers for an online discussion board
- Shakespeare's *Hamlet*, the play, and possibly a film adaptation, such as one of the following:

    Hamlet (1948) directed by Lawrence Olivier

    Hamle, (1964) starring Richard Burton; directed by Bill Colleran and John Gielgud.

    Hamlet (1964) directed by Grigori Kozintsev

    Hamlet, Prince of Denmark (1980) (BBC-TV) starring Patrick Stewart and directed by Rodney Bennett

    Hamlet (1991) directed by Franco Zeffirelli

    Hamlet (1996) starring Kenneth Branagh, Richard Attenborough, Judi Dench, Billy Crystal, and Kate Winslet; directed by Kenneth Branagh

    Hamlet (2000) starring Ethan Hawke, Julia Stiles, and Kyle MacLachlan; directed by Michael Almereyda

Process/Procedure

1. Assign each student a particular character to follow in the play.
2. Whether the students read the play or watch a film, remind them to pay particular attention to their characters' lines.

3. Discuss the play in class—either in groups or as a class.

4. Post a prompt or questions to the discussion board to be answered as homework. Sample prompt:

> Hamlet is bringing Claudius to trial for killing his father. As your character, what would you say if you were put on the witness stand? Give a quote to justify your response. Then respond to at least two of your classmates' postings.

Pointers or Pitfalls

Depending upon the age of the students, reading *Hamlet* can be difficult and may require outside interpretation. Students tend to want to answer without thinking; that is why the reference to quotations in the play is important. If this is the first discussion board in a class, students will probably need some assistance with computer technology.

Ponderings

Students enjoy the creativity of this activity and the opportunity to view various adaptations of the play on film. The exercise engages students and forces them to read and listen closely and critically.

LESSON 44
FINDING SHAKESPEARE: APPLICATION AND ANALYSIS

Susan S. Hawkes

Purpose

- To extend exposure to Shakespeare's plays
- To apply knowledge in individual analysis

Preparation

- Notes and film on Renaissance Theater and William Shakespeare
- In-class reading and discussion of any Shakespearean play

Props/Materials

- Text of chosen play (each student selects a different play)
- Shakespeare Project instruction sheet (Figure 3.13)
- Shakespeare Project Checklist (Figure 3.14)
- Literature Oral Report Evaluation (Figure 3.15)
- Model of "Dear Parent" Progress Letter (Figure 3.16)

Process/Procedure

Instruct students to select the Shakespearean play they wish to read. Distribute and review the Shakespeare Project Instruction sheet. Distribute the Shakespeare Project Checklist on the day rough drafts are checked. Designate specific days to work on projects in class and due dates for reports.

Pointers or Pitfalls

In higher-level classes, each student should work with a different play; in average classes, students may work with a partner; in low-level classes, this activity can be a group project. Prepare a sign-up sheet to avoid conflict over play choices. Review documentation of quotes and tell students that it's acceptable to use CliffsNotes—they will anyway— as long as they document carefully.

Ponderings

Be sure students have access to notes given in class, especially for absentees, and provide sample news articles to demonstrate that the Shakespearean Chronicles (see Figure 3.13) are more than summaries of the plays.

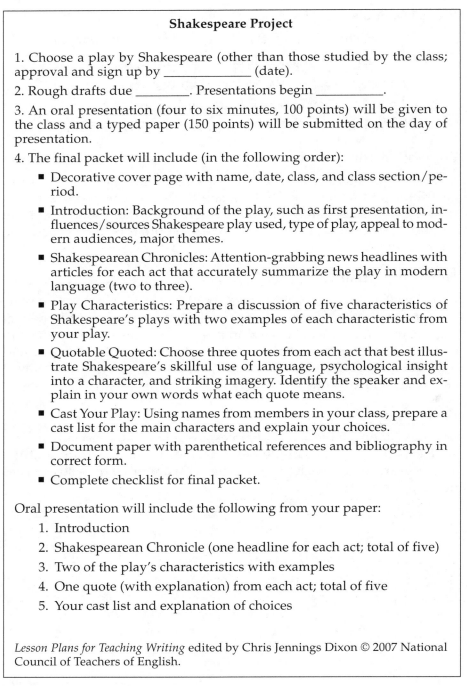

Shakespeare Project

1. Choose a play by Shakespeare (other than those studied by the class; approval and sign up by _____ (date).

2. Rough drafts due _____. Presentations begin _____.

3. An oral presentation (four to six minutes, 100 points) will be given to the class and a typed paper (150 points) will be submitted on the day of presentation.

4. The final packet will include (in the following order):

 ▪ Decorative cover page with name, date, class, and class section/period.

 ▪ Introduction: Background of the play, such as first presentation, influences/sources Shakespeare play used, type of play, appeal to modern audiences, major themes.

 ▪ Shakespearean Chronicles: Attention-grabbing news headlines with articles for each act that accurately summarize the play in modern language (two to three).

 ▪ Play Characteristics: Prepare a discussion of five characteristics of Shakespeare's plays with two examples of each characteristic from your play.

 ▪ Quotable Quoted: Choose three quotes from each act that best illustrate Shakespeare's skillful use of language, psychological insight into a character, and striking imagery. Identify the speaker and explain in your own words what each quote means.

 ▪ Cast Your Play: Using names from members in your class, prepare a cast list for the main characters and explain your choices.

 ▪ Document paper with parenthetical references and bibliography in correct form.

 ▪ Complete checklist for final packet.

Oral presentation will include the following from your paper:

 1. Introduction

 2. Shakespearean Chronicle (one headline for each act; total of five)

 3. Two of the play's characteristics with examples

 4. One quote (with explanation) from each act; total of five

 5. Your cast list and explanation of choices

Lesson Plans for Teaching Writing edited by Chris Jennings Dixon © 2007 National Council of Teachers of English.

Figure 3.13

Shakespeare Project Checklist

Use the following checklist to be sure you have followed directions and included all parts of the project:

1. Does your cover page have . . . ?
Play title _____   Class _____   Date_____
Name _____   Period _____   Creative décor___

2. Does your introduction have . . . ?
Date of first presentation ____   Type of play ____   Major themes____
Sources/influences ____   Audience appeal ___
Documentation (parenthetical references) ___

3. Do your "news" articles have . . . ?
Attention-grabbing headlines____   Accurate play information ____
Journalistic style writing ____   Two or three articles for each act ____
Attractive/creative presentation____

4. Have you selected . . . ?
Five play characteristics ___
Two examples for each characteristic, identified by act and scene ____

5. Did you . . . ?
Select three quotes from each act ____   Explain each quote ____
Document quotes (act, scene, line) ____

6. Does your cast list . . . ?
Use class members ____   Explain each choice ___
Cast only main characters____

7. Do you have a bibliography . . . ?
Of all sources used ____ In correct format ___ In alphabetical order ___

8. Did you . . . ?
Proofread/edit carefully ____   Type your project ____
Have at least one other person and/or a parent read your project ____

9. Does your final project . . . ?
Contain all sections required in a large envelope that closes ____
Cover page ___   Play characteristics ____
Introduction ___   Quotable quotes ____
Shakespearean Chronicles ___   Cast list and explanation ___

10. Did you . . . ?
Follow all directions in the order given ____
Use at least twelve-point font ___
Use only block style for narrative parts ____

Lesson Plans for Teaching Writing edited by Chris Jennings Dixon © 2007 National Council of Teachers of English.

Figure 3.14

Literature Oral Report Evaluation

Shakespearean Project

Presenter: Play Title:

Introduction:

     Date of first presentation: Type of play:

     Sources/influences:

     Major themes: Audience appeal:

Shakespearean Chronicles
     Headlines:
          Act 1—
          Act 2—
          Act 3—
          Act 4—
          Act 5—

     Accurate play information (Yes____No____)

Play Characteristics and Examples
        1.
        2.

Quotes with Explanations
        1.
        2.
        3.
        4.
        5.

Delivery

     Strongest factor:

     Weakest factor:

Lesson Plans for Teaching Writing edited by Chris Jennings Dixon © 2007 National
Council of Teachers of English.

Figure 3.15

Progress Letter

DATE

Dear Parent(s),

Research papers for my English classes are due on Day of Week, DATE. In March, each student gave a PowerPoint presentation and was told at that time some of the same information would be used to complete a research paper. In April, students were given an assignment sheet with specific instructions and due dates for their final papers. Students have been working on the preliminary steps in and out of class for two weeks, and this has been the only assignment. Each preliminary step counts as a grade, and the final paper counts as three test grades.

To date, _____ has not submitted the following assignments:

_____ preliminary bibliography   _____documented rough draft
_____ preliminary outline   _____typed final copy
_____ note cards

It is essential that all preliminary work and the final paper be completed according to instructions and submitted on or before the deadline given in order to avoid failure for this grading period. All preliminary work must be submitted in the final package. Please encourage your child to comply with these requirements as outlined on the assignment sheet.

As a reminder, students will be taking the reading/literature/research part of the state mandated tests on DATE. They should be present, well rested, and prepared to do their best.

Please call me at school (PHONE NUMBER; TIME) if you have questions. Thank you for your support.

Sincerely,

English Teacher

Lesson Plans for Teaching Writing edited by Chris Jennings Dixon © 2007 National Council of Teachers of English.

Figure 3.16

IV Research

"Yikes! The Research Paper Unit!" Despite the moaning and groaning by students and, sometimes, teachers, research skills continue to be an important focus of composition in secondary and postsecondary classrooms. This section provides practical approaches to all stages of the research paper—from generation of a thesis to investigation and evaluation of sources and through drafting, revising, and editing. To promote an understanding of basic research principals and to assist students in becoming knowledgeable consumers of research, the overall focus of these activities is on the process rather than the product. Activities provide ample opportunities for students to generate meaningful research for diverse writing purposes.

LESSON 45
PIZZA CAROUSEL: DEMONSTRATING
READING/RESEARCH SKILLS

Regina D. Taylor

Purpose

- To demonstrate reading comprehension and research skills

Preparation

The teacher divides chapters or sections of a text into assignments for group work.

Props/Materials

- Pizza Carousel handout (Figure 4.1)
- Construction paper
- Markers, scissors, rulers
- Empty pizza boxes, if available

Process/Procedure

1. Teacher assigns a chapter or section of the current class reading to groups composed of six students.

2. Using construction paper, students draw an outer circle with six inner segments (or slices), like a pizza pie, creating bigger pieces for those slices that will contain more information.

3. Students determine how each member of the group will assume responsibility for completing responses on the six pizza segments.

4. Students number pizza segments/slices on the back and then cut out and distribute them to the group members.

5. Students provide responses on their individual pizza segments/slices for their assigned readings using the following prompts:
   - Identify group members' names and roles.
   - Note assigned chapter number.

- Write a chapter summary.
- Provide an illustration of main scene with a brief description.
- Answers chapter questions (as generated by teacher).
- Give two definitions of literary terms with illustrations as found in assigned chapter.

6. After completing the responses, group members tape the pizza segments/slices together and then present the whole pizza to the class.

7. Teacher continuously monitors students as they respond to their assignments and then prepare and present their responses.

Pointers or Pitfalls

Be sure to pace the students by directing them to complete certain tasks on certain dates. Also assign the individual prompts as homework on the first day so students return to class prepared to work on and complete their projects. The assignment may be varied to allow students to self-select chapters for their group work, but be sure to coordinate their choices among all groups. Do not allow the slices or segments to leave the classroom, as the group experience is one that can only be recreated in the classroom environment.

Ponderings

The students who have difficulty putting the pizza back together after cutting it into segments are usually the ones who have forgotten to number the backsides of their slices.

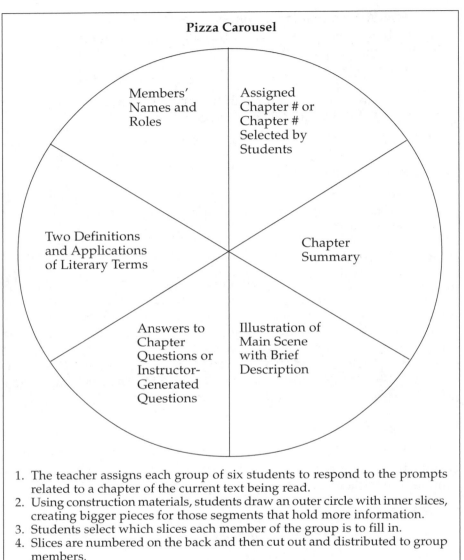

Pizza Carousel

Members' Names and Roles

Assigned Chapter # or Chapter # Selected by Students

Two Definitions and Applications of Literary Terms

Chapter Summary

Answers to Chapter Questions or Instructor-Generated Questions

Illustration of Main Scene with Brief Description

1. The teacher assigns each group of six students to respond to the prompts related to a chapter of the current text being read.
2. Using construction materials, students draw an outer circle with inner slices, creating bigger pieces for those segments that hold more information.
3. Students select which slices each member of the group is to fill in.
4. Slices are numbered on the back and then cut out and distributed to group members.
5. Students respond to prompts on each segment of the pie by writing information on their slices.
6. When all group members have completed their segments, the slices are taped back together and the whole pizza pie is presented to the class.
7. The teacher observes students completing responses and presenting their chapter assignments.

Lesson Plans for Teaching Writing edited by Chris Jennings Dixon © 2007 National Council of Teachers of English.

Figure 4.1

LESSON 46
AMTRAK SCHEDULE: USING PRIMARY SOURCES

Suzy S. Bolton

Purpose

- To practice finding factual details from a primary source
- To demonstrate how to incorporate information into basic responses

Preparation

Preparation is minimal. This is a "throw off the end of a pier" activity used to introduce a concept. It works well as an introductory activity for research as it gives a realistic prompt for students to read primary sources to obtain factual data.

Props/Materials

- Amtrak Train Schedule (available as a bulletin from local Amtrak station or on website at www.amtrak.com/servlet/ContentServer?pagename=Amtrak/HomePage)
- Amtrak Schedule Activity handout (Figure 4.2)

Process/Procedure

1. Teacher passes out a sample train schedule and then explains how students can find a specific train departure time.
2. Teacher distributes copies of Amtrak Train Schedule handout and asks students to answer questions on the form.
3. Students are given thirty minutes to respond to the questions and to write a one-paragraph plan for taking a trip using the Amtrak schedule.
4. Teacher concludes lesson with a discussion of how students can continue to use primary sources to give them authority as writers.

Pointers or Pitfalls

The schedule that I have used is for local transportation in my area. The questions in the handout may be adapted to transportation schedules in your area. This activity works especially well with low-level learners. You may want to have students work in groups rather than independently. Assigning students to complete the activity individually or as a group may depend on the nature of the class or on the need to vary class structure for variety.

Ponderings

Students gain confidence in their ability to work with a primary source that has real-life significance. They also feel as if they have gained a practical skill while learning to integrate basic research into a written response.

Amtrak Schedule Activity

Using the train schedule provided, answer the following questions:

1. What train number arrives daily at the Richmond, Virginia, Staples Mill Road Station at 12:57 P.M.?

2. What is the name of the train that leaves Boston's South Station at 5:15 A.M. and arrives in Washington, D.C., at 11:47 A.M.?

3. What is the symbol that is used to indicate that first-class service is available on a train?

4. What on-board services are available on train #91?

5. What days of operation apply to train #2153?

6. What does the "C" indicate in train #2153's days of operation?

Now, plan a trip using the train schedule:

1. Tell the date and time of departure
2. Give the train number and destination
3. What services will you enjoy on your trip?
4. How long will you stay?
5. When and how will you return?

Write the above answers into a single paragraph.

Lesson Plans for Teaching Writing edited by Chris Jennings Dixon © 2007 National Council of Teachers of English.

Figure 4.2

LESSON 47
WEBSITES: EVALUATING AUTHORITY

Marty Brooks

Purpose

- To identify criteria to evaluate the authority of sites on the Internet
- To determine the authority of Internet sites using criteria of credibility, accuracy, reasonableness, and support

Preparation

This exercise is most beneficial before students conduct research on the Internet. Present the criteria to be used: credibility, accuracy, reasonableness, and support. Review the terms with the class and discuss real-life examples.

Props/Materials

- Teacher and students need access to computers and to the Internet
- Evaluating Internet Sources handout (Figure 4.3)

Process/Procedure

1. After introducing the concept of "authority" and discussing the qualities that a reader expects for a text to be authoritative, the teacher notes that the Internet presents specific challenges for a researcher who is trying to determine a text's authority, such as a lack of background information on the site creator.

2. Teacher distributes Evaluating Internet Sources handout and asks students to surf to the first site listed— site on evaluating internet sources.

3. Students review the site and list four qualities that might be used to determine a text's authority.

4. Students work individually to complete the remaining exercises on the handout. (This takes approximately forty minutes.)

5. After all students have examined the sites and responded to the questions, students share their findings and present justifications for their responses.

Pointers or Pitfalls

You need to check the websites listed on the handout to be sure they are still posted. You also may want to vary the websites or focus them on one subject, such as the greenhouse effect, or a topic that you are studying in class. I picked the sites for this handout because they show the multiple ways that sites structure documentation and give information about the Web sponsors and writers. For instance, *Slate* articles, referring to studies or facts, often have hypertext links that take the reader to the original article where the study or fact is found. Monitor student progress to help students push past the basic information. For instance, point out to students that some sites are checked by Web accreditation organizations.

Ponderings

Despite students' experience with and reliance on the Internet, they often have difficulty checking the authority of a site, and they are surprised that they have been reading and using sites for so long without noticing the sponsor information that is uncovered in this activity. This is a wonderful exercise for making students see the Internet from a different, more critical, angle.

Evaluating Internet Sources

Go to the following address and read the information given on the page: www.virtualsalt.com/evalu8it.htm

Print out the CARS checklist.

Now, evaluate the following websites to determine if you would trust the information given and if they are "authoritative."

Source 1
http://slate.msn.com
Choose any article in *Slate* magazine. List the following information: author's name, author's title or position; author's organizational affiliation, date of page creation or version, author's contact information.
　　Is this a good source for information? Note why or why not. You will want to use the "Credibility, Accuracy, Reasonableness, and Support" criteria to answer this.

Source 2
www.findserenitynow.com/index.html?1368
Look through this website on depression. List the following information: author's name, author's title or position; author's organizational affiliation, date of page creation or version, author's contact information.
　　Is this a good source for information? Note why or why not. You will want to use the "Credibility, Accuracy, Reasonableness, and Support" criteria to answer this.

Source 3
health.yahoo.com/health/centers/depression/32131.html
Look through this website on depression. List the following information: author's name, author's title or position; author's organizational affiliation, date of page creation or version, author's contact information.
　　Is this a good source for information? Note why or why not. You will want to use the "Credibility, Accuracy, Reasonableness, and Support" criteria to answer this question.

Source 4
www.historyandtheory.org/
Choose any article in *History and Theory*. List the following information: author's name, author's title or position; author's organizational affiliation, date of page creation or version, author's contact information.
　　Is this a good source for information? Note why or why not. You will want to use the "Credibility, Accuracy, Reasonableness, and Support" criteria to answer this question.

Rank the four above sites in order of reliability.

Lesson Plans for Teaching Writing edited by Chris Jennings Dixon © 2007 National Council of Teachers of English.

Figure 4.3

LESSON 48
MINE: RECOGNIZING THE LINE BETWEEN WRITER AND SOURCE

Reginald Bruster

Purpose

- To gather information from multiple sources and avoid plagiarism
- To take notes using source information and writer reflection

Preparation

Students read information about Modern Language Association (MLA) documentation and how to use the reference library in their writing handbooks. The teacher reviews the "how" and "why" for documentation to ensure that students have been exposed to the basics of parenthetical citing.

Props/Materials

5" x 8" lined index cards (a pack of twenty-five)
Sample Note-Taking Cards handout (Figure 4.4)

Process/Procedure

1. The teacher emphasizes a few preliminary points:
   - Borrow sparingly from sources
   - Borrow a single piece of information for each index card

2. The teacher instructs:
   - When you first consult a source, write the MLA bibliographical information on the first line. Do this for each new source.
   - Attribute a letter to the source in the upper right corner of the card. This source will be called source A. Each time you borrow information from source A, put the letter A in the upper right corner. You don't need to rewrite the bibliographical information as you have already done so with the first card for source A.

- Borrow the information from the source verbatim and cite parenthetically. Remember to enclose quotations in quotation marks.

- Draw a line below the verbatim borrowed information and under that line write in capital letters the word MINE. The "mine" part of the note-taking process is your reflection on the value of the verbatim borrowed information to your thesis. The "mine" section also shows the researcher how he or might use the borrowed information.

3. Students are encouraged to write the thesis statements on separate 5" x 8" cards and keep those with them as they gather information on their note cards. Better, students should write their preliminary outlines to help guide their research gathering.

4. Students are forewarned that the research process demands different ways of thinking than the actual writing of the paper. Students sift through their sources to identify "borrowed" information relevant to their topics of research.

5. Students identify "borrowed information" as distinct from their own reflections and ideas with this note-taking method.

6. The teacher guides students in the note-taking procedure using note card samples, such as shown in Figure 4.4.

Pointers or Pitfalls

Because research is gathering information and presenting it as a whole, students often have difficulty with plagiarism in the initial stages of research. The goal for this method of note taking is to help students insert borrowed information into their work without plagiarizing. The sample cards allow students a few choices as to how they will use the borrowed information. Since students have written the borrowed information verbatim, they can choose to use it verbatim or paraphrase or use parts of a source. Most likely, they will insert the borrowed information (in bold) into their "mine" section. Hence, their text may read as such:

> Denying colonized people the right to speak their native tongue in their own country or community disempowers

them. They become subjugated victims of an outsider who validates himself by invalidating everything having to do with victims. Hence, when the invader imposes his language as the new native tongue, he forces natives to change the way they operate (thinking, speaking, social relationships, identity, etc.) as a society. A good example of this kind of colonial impact on natives is the Britain's colonization. **"So many peoples formerly colonized by Britain [. . .] speak English, write in English, use English in their schools and universities, and conduct government business in English. [This use of English demonstrates] the residual effect of colonial domination on their cultures"** (Tyson 365).

Ponderings

In the second note taken on Grace Paley's story "Samuel" in Figure 4.4, the writer has borrowed from the verbatim information in the "mine" section. The "mine" section allows students to remember their reason for taking the note, an important aspect of research. Because this note card is an example of APA bibliographic citation, the teacher will need to explain to students that the MLA is not the only style for preparing note cards.

Sample Note-Taking Cards

An example of an MLA bibliographic citation.

Thesis: Language used as a weapon to control the colonized and safeguard the welfare of the colonizer is a significant aspect in postcolonial theory.

A

Tyson, Lois. *Critical Theory Today: A User-Friendly Guide.* Vol. 2070. New York: Garland, 1999.

"That so many peoples formerly colonized by Britain, in addition to the local languages they may use at home, speak English, write in English, use English in their schools and universities, and conduct government business in English is an indication of the residual effect of colonial domination on their cultures" (365).

MINE: Denying people the right to speak their native tongue in their own country or community disempowers them. They become subjugated victims of an outsider who validates himself by invalidating everything having to do with victims. Hence, when the invader imposes his language as the new native tongue, he forces natives to change the way they operate (thinking, speaking, social relationships, identity, etc.) as a society.

An example of American Psychological Association bibliographic citation.

Thesis: Masculinity defined solely as performance encourages and rewards violence.

B

Paley, Grace. (2001). "Samuel." In Laurie G. Kirszner & Stephen R. Mandell (Eds.), *Patterns of college writing: A rhetorical reader and guide* (pp. 212–214). Boston: Bedford/St. Martin's.

"Some boys are very tough. They're afraid of nothing. They are the ones who climb a wall and take a bow at the top" (2001, p. 212).

MINE: Grace Paley's introduction in her story "Samuel" captures what could be called the masculine manifesto: that being tough and fearless assures applause and praise. This manifesto manifests only when males do something, when a boy, for example, "climb[s] a wall and take[s] a bow at the top" (2001, p. 212) because he has succeeded in performing a feat dangerous enough to warrant his male peers' praise and admiration. He bows to expressions of awe and shock that affirm his success in upholding rigid standards of masculinity.

Lesson Plans for Teaching Writing edited by Chris Jennings Dixon © 2007 National Council of Teachers of English.

Figure 4.4

LESSON 49
CREATING A LITERATE LIFESTYLE:
FORMING READING AND WRITING HABITS

Jennifer Fletcher

Purpose

- To reflect and rethink attitudes about daily literacy
- To acquire lifelong reading and writing habits

Preparation

Most high school students have difficulty making time for independent reading and writing within their busy schedules. However, writers and researchers know that a literate lifestyle is essential to the high levels of inquiry and critical thinking required by college-level course work. In other words, students must form a *habit* of reading and writing in order to conduct and analyze original research. The following activity encourages students to imagine themselves as independent scholars. Reproduce enough daily schedules for each student; make an overhead transparency of the top five lists and Quickwrite prompt.

Props/Materials

- Overhead transparencies
- Yearlong Research Project Checkpoint List handout (Figure 4.5)

Process/Procedure

1. Using an overhead transparency, the teacher models a typical student day by soliciting class responses.

2. The teacher directs students to individually list their current activities (all course work, extracurricular activities, meals, homework, leisure pastime) in an hourly schedule from 5 A.M. to 11 P.M. (If students state that their schedules vary from day to day, ask them to list activities for a typical day.)

3. The teacher informs students that most authors and researchers find daily reading and writing produce the greatest amount and highest quality of written work.

4. Using the original hourly schedule from 5 A.M. to 11 P.M. developed for a typical day, the teacher overlaps the original transparency to model changes in a daily schedule to plan time for more reading and writing.

5. The teacher assigns students to accommodate an additional hour of independent (i.e., not assigned) reading and writing. Students must still allow themselves eight hours of sleep.

6. Students maintain logs over a stated time period during which they make plans for reading and writing.

7. After students have implemented their revised daily schedules, they meet in pair-share groups to discuss the changes they are actually making in their schedules.

8. The teacher guides students in sharing the challenges they face in creating a more literate lifestyle. (Five minutes)

9. The teacher assigns students to inventory "Five Things You Like to Read" and "Five Things You Like to Write."

10. From these inventories, students are directed to Quickwrite (five minutes) from the prompt:

    "What will be the greatest challenge you will face in creating a literate lifestyle?" and "What are some resources than can help?"

11. Teacher assigns the Yearlong Research Project and reviews the checklist with students.

12. Teacher and students regularly monitor individual student progress using Yearlong Research Project Checklist (handout).

    Note: This assignment requires cooperation among all teachers in the department to ensure that students complete the requirements even if they are transferred from one class to another.

13. Students showcase their skills in reading multiple sources and writing their research papers over a yearlong period.

Pointers or Pitfalls

This activity can be an engaging and personal way for each student to begin a major research project. Students often are grateful for the opportunity to talk about the difficult demands and pressures of their daily schedules. While this lesson gives each student the opportunity to begin exploring different time management strategies and attitudes toward scholarship, multiple follow-up activities are necessary before most students make the leap from recognizing the importance of daily literacy to developing a compelling habit of reading and writing.

Ponderings

Those students who most successfully completed their Yearlong Research Projects do indeed reflect the literacy behaviors of independent scholars. These students learn to use *unassigned* Quickwrites to clarify their thinking, seek and enthusiastically read multiple sources on their topics, and consult teachers and peers for feedback on their work. Many of these students treat their projects as their hobby—reading texts from their field and exceeding the minimum requirements of the research assignment. The key to these students' successes lies in the unusual length of time allowed for them to develop scholarly habits. Because the students have seven months to complete their projects, they enjoy the luxury of refining their topics, changing their arguments, reading sources extraneous to their final papers, engaging in impromptu discussions of their topics, and enjoying serendipitous discoveries while in other classes and contexts—behaviors common to university researchers but rare in most high school students.

Yearlong Research Project Checkpoint List

The following checkpoint dates are nonnegotiable. Your work MUST be ready to turn in on these days in order to receive full credit for the checkpoint. These dates are the same regardless of your English teacher. In the event of a schedule change, you are still responsible for the completion of the checkpoints as well as the final research paper.

Checkpoint 1   **Due Date:**
- Commitment Paper
- "Why I Chose My Topic and What I Hope to Learn" (two double-spaced pages)
- What is your topic?
- Why have you chosen it?
- What do you already know about it?
- What do you hope to learn about it?

Checkpoint 2   **Due Date:**
- Use five sources in proper Works Cited format on your topic.
- Include sources using books, magazines, Internet articles, personal interviews, newspapers, etc.
- Record publishing information to prepare index cards and a Works Cited sheet.
- These sources are a bare minimum. More sources need to be used to receive a higher grade.
- Read and highlight one periodical source to identify significant information.

Checkpoint 3   **Due Date:**
- Read and highlight a second periodical source to identify significant information.
- Provide documentation of an interview with a competent person in the field of your research.
- Develop a working thesis statement.

.**Checkpoint 4**   **Due Date:**
- Write a two-page summary of information gathered so far.
- Write a prospectus for additional research.

Checkpoint 5   **Due Date:**
- Read and highlight a third periodical source to identify significant information.
- Write a full sentence outline.

Checkpoint 6   **Due Date:**
- Final checkpoint.
- Write a five- to seven-page final draft research paper.
- Present a plan for showcasing your presentation.

NOTE: Failure to turn in a final project will result in failure for the second semester.

Lesson Plans for Teaching Writing edited by Chris Jennings Dixon © 2007 National Council of Teachers of English.

Figure 4.5

LESSON 50
SELF-WRITING DIAGNOSIS: REVISION STRATEGIES

Elizabeth H. Beagle

Purpose

- To develop skill in self-diagnosis in identification of areas in need of improvement
- To practice self-assessment strategies for revision

Preparation

Collect and evaluate student analysis/research papers. Instead of making editing marks and annotated comments about student weakness or errors in writing, highlight the words and/or sentences that require revision. Additionally, assign a score indicating student skill in the following areas: (1) composition and usage, (2) use of MLA bibliographic style guide, and (3) analysis.

Props/Materials

- Directions for Self-Writing Diagnosis handout (Figure 4.6)
- Writing handbook
- List of online writing lab resources
  (The Writing Center at the University of Maine provides numerous examples at www.ume.maine.edu/~wcenter/others.html)

Process/Procedure

1. Review the scoring system with students prior to returning their highlighted research papers.

2. Distribute copies of Directions for Self-Writing Diagnosis handout to each student.

3. Instruct students to review their papers to determine what in the highlighted areas needs to be improved.

4. Provide an example from outside this class to illustrate the process of self-diagnosis. The example may be written on a transparency or on the board.

5. Encourage students to use the writing center, Internet sites, and their writing handbooks for assistance in diagnosing errors highlighted on their research papers.

6. Guide students to not only correct their mistakes but to also write written explanations for each error.

7. Instruct students to use the teacher as their last resort for answers.

8. Require students to resubmit their papers with their self-corrections and explanations. (This may be used as a separate grade.)

Pointers or Pitfalls

Students may be reluctant to diagnosis their own errors. They usually want to conference with the teacher as "the easy way out" instead of trying to find the explanations for the errors themselves. Remind the students that you, as the teacher, are trying to enforce a life skill, one that they can use to correct their own mistakes.

Ponderings

This is a wonderful activity that can be adjusted for any written assignment. Once the students realize that the teacher is not going to give them the answers, they usually develop a growing sense of confidence in their ability to analyze and correct their own errors.

Directions for Self-Writing Diagnosis

Look over your scoring guide for your research paper. For each score lower than three, complete the information requested. If there is an area in which you scored a three or lower that is not listed here, include it in "Other." If you cannot figure out what is wrong, use your writing handbook or one of the following electronic resources.

> www.MLA.org
> http://owl.english.purdue.edu
> http://www.ume.maine.edu/~wcenter/others.html

Composition and Usage
- Clear, concise thesis statement   Score:
  1. Problem: Resource Used:
  2. Correction:
- Elaborated with layers of detail (not exhaustively) Score:
  1. Problem: Resource Used:
  2. Correction:

Use of MLA style guide
- Appropriate use of internal citations   Score:
  1. Problem: Resource Used:
  2. Correction:
- Adequate works-cited page   Score:
  1. Problem: Resource Used:
  2. Correction:
- Research is suitable to prove thesis   Score:
  1. Problem: Resource Used:
  2. Correction:
- Notes/outline/rough draft   Score:
  1. Problem: Resource Used:
  2. Correction:

Analysis
- Not a summary   Score:
  1. Problem: Resource Used:
  2. Correction:
- Appropriate/adequate quotes from primary text   Score:
  1. Problem: Resource Used:
  2. Correction:
- Addresses single piece of literature   Score:
  1. Problem: Resource Used:
  2. Correction:
- Focuses on one or more elements of literature   Score:
  1. Problem: Resource Used:
  2. Correction:

Other
  1. Problem   Score:
  2. Correction   Resource Used:

Lesson Plans for Teaching Writing edited by Chris Jennings Dixon © 2007 National Council of Teachers of English.

Figure 4.6

LESSON 51
"WHAT SHOULD SALLY DO?" AVOIDING PLAGIARISM

Charles S. Pierce Jr.

Purpose

- To reflect on the definition of plagiarism
- To construct strategies to avoid confrontations about plagiarism

Preparation

The teacher writes on the board or distributes copies of the given scenario about a plagiarism situation. (The given scenario may be adapted for your students. Be ready for student questions about the scenario.) This activity is also a good one to conduct in a computer lab.

Props/Materials

Prepare copies of a scenario depicting student reaction to a teacher's evaluation of writing that contains plagiarism. The following scenario may be used:

> Sally Student receives a paper back from Professor I. M. Wise. He has written at the top of the paper that Sally will receive a zero on the paper and an F on the course because of plagiarism in her paper. He also has marked two passages that he says are plagiarized and added the comment, "The first two passages are word for word from Smith. . . ." He then circles a passage and says "This passage seems highly indebted to Jones. Both the wording and the idea are similar." Finally, he adds that due to a lack of quotations and documentation of any kind for these passages, plagiarism clearly exists in the paper. As a result, Professor Wise says that he plans to refer the paper to the dean of students and ask him to maintain a file on Sally so that if plagiarism occurs again she will be expelled from the college.

Process/Procedure

1. Students read the scenario.

2. Students may break the sequence of their responses into answers to the following: What should Sally do? In what order? What should be her goal? What will provide the best outcome for Sally? For the teacher?

3. The teacher encourages students to think about additional aspects of the problem, such as:

   - Did Sally really plagiarize?

   - What does the student handbook say about plagiarism, and is it mentioned in the course outline?

   - What lack of knowledge or carelessness caused the plagiarism?

   - Should Sally approach Professor I. M. Wise and try to head off the problem?

   - What should she say and what should be her attitude?

4. Students should present various options and suggestions and weigh the value of each response.

5. Using their immediate as well as thought-out responses, each student writes one-paragraph telling Sally what to do! (About six to ten sentences.)

6. Students should be told that their answers will be graded on reasoning, content, organization, sentence structure, word choice, and mechanics.

7. Students should also be reminded to write for their audience.

8. Finally, students need to be reminded that what they are seeking is a solution that will be satisfactory for Sally— and her teacher.

Pointers or Pitfalls

This activity should be assigned as an in-class interactive exercise where students can talk about what they might do and how they could help each other. If possible, arrange for the class to meet in a computer lab to easily monitor, listen, and look at drafts.

Ponderings

Preferably, each student develops a one-paragraph response, but it is also possible to have a group of about four students work on the assignment together. This assignment may also be done at home. Surprisingly, this assignment is very difficult for many students. Some want to blame the teacher for the problem. (Are we surprised?) Others want Sally to give up and just accept an F for the course. Most never think to look at the course outline or the student handbook. Finally, students need to be told that answers like "talk to the teacher" are not adequate, because the reader needs to know more specifically what the student might do or say to win over the teacher. Thus, if the teacher makes this an in-class exercise, preferably in the computer lab, students who are having difficulty with the activity may be observed, and the teacher may want to drop hints about some sensible actions to take.

V Grammar

"How do we engage our students in grammar studies?" Although the technical, rule-driven, grammatical approach to composition is often frowned upon by writing process theorists, teachers know they must prepare their students to write compositions that demonstrate a basic understanding and control of sentence structure, word usage, and Standard Written English. Discarding traditional drill approaches, teacher-contributors in this section encourage students to self-diagnose their technical strengths and weaknesses and develop prescriptions for personal writing improvement. Interestingly enough, many of these strategies have been developed in college classrooms in response to students' lack of preparation for college composition. This section contains visual and textual approaches to mastering the mechanics of writing. The activities describe strategies that motivate students to assess and refine their writing practices.

LESSON 52
"I'M NOT GOOD AT ENGLISH": EIGHT BASIC RULES FOR NATIVE SPEAKERS

Reginald Bruster

Purpose

- To develop skills in constructing sentences through an innate understanding of language
- To practice sentence construction and punctuation using eight basic rules

Preparation

This activity helps native speakers of English who struggle with grammar and punctuation to interact with basic premises of language. The teacher needs to present two terms for this discourse: *sentence* and *nonsentence*. It is not necessary to throw a lot of terms at students—e.g., relative clause, adverbial clause, etc. Students need to be able to locate the subject and verb of a sentence. The rule for recognizing a *declarative sentence* depends on students' innate understanding of their language.

Props/Materials

Eight Basic Rules of Punctuation handout (Figure 5.1)

Process/Procedure

1. Distribute the Eight Basic Rules of Punctuation handout and review each one with the class.

   Note: There are three ways that nonsentences (fragments) interact with sentences. A nonsentence introduces a sentence, interrupts a sentence, and/or comes after a sentence.

2. Explain that anything that is not a sentence is called a nonsentence. You may want to mention terms such as "fragment," "comma splice," and "fused sentence or run-on sentence" because these are terms students see marked on their papers and hear in composition classes.

3. Introduce the following formula as a way for students to check their sentences for completion: *"They didn't know that _____."* (Any pronoun will suffice for the subject.)

4. Then provide two examples for students to determine if either word group is a fragment or nonsentence:

>   a. "Although I went to the store."
>
>   b. "I didn't buy anything."

5. Instruct students to use the given formula with the examples as provided:

>   a. "They didn't know that <u>although I went to the store</u>." The native speaker will hear incompleteness in this sentence.
>
>   b. "They didn't know that <u>I didn't</u> <u>buy anything</u>." The native speaker will hear completeness in this sentence.

6. If students are unsure whether a sentence is complete or not, ask them to use the questionable sentence in the blank of the formula. If the questionable sentence makes sense as a part of the formula's sentence, then the questionable sentence is probably a sentence. If the questionable sentence does not make sense, it is probably a fragment or nonsentence.

7. Provide several examples during the class discussion.

8. Review the eight basic rules and then test students to determine their mastery of the rules.

Pointers or Pitfalls

The goal of this lesson is to ease, if not eliminate, fears and uncertainties about speaking English. Students can use their innate understanding of language with the eight basic rules. Here is another example I have used. Ask a student a question in which he or she must use the subordinating conjunction "because" to begin his or her response.

>   *Teacher:* Why did you choose College X for your education?
>
>   *Student:* Because College X's nursing program is reputable among hospitals.
>
>   (The teacher writes the response on the board.)
>
>   *Teacher (to the class):* Did anyone misunderstand Kelly's response?
>
>   (Class says "No.")
>
>   *Teacher:* In everyday, nonstandard usage, responses like this are accepted and understood. But if we place the

response in our formula to check for sentence completion, we see that the response is a fragment or nonsentence.

(Use the formula here. Then explain how the fragment or nonsentence can be corrected using the information from the context of the dialogue.)

Teacher: All we need to do to make this nonsentence a sentence is to give it a closing.

(The teacher writes the correction on the board.)

"Because College X's nursing program is reputable among hospitals, Kelley enrolled at College X." (Once students see the revision, the class can discuss more succinct revisions.)

Ponderings

Since native speakers' problems with grammar and punctuation differ from nonnative speakers who may learn English prescriptively, native speakers often need to rely on their innate understandings and relationships with their language. I discuss native speakers' intimacy with English so that students do not feel so distant from Standard English. Those students who say "I'm not good in English" or "English is my worst subject" are challenged when they realize that they know English better than they think.

By getting students to redefine how they think about their English, I ask them to discard the notion that they speak incorrect English and suggest that they use the term *nonstandard* English instead. *Incorrect* connotes that the type of speech used in a given context is ineffective for communicating. Since speech is often done within communities that use a certain type of nonstandard English to communicate within that community, speech is not incorrect or ineffective. For example, hip-hop slang communicates effectively within hip-hop communities. Yet hip-hop, like all nonstandard usage, recontextualizes (or revises) Standard English. Hence, nonstandard usage can be revised to standard usage.

Eight Basic Rules of Punctuation

1. Sentence. Sentence.
   e.g., "I went to the store. I didn't buy anything."

2. Sentence, *for* sentence.
   > *and*
   > *nor*
   > *but*
   > *or*
   > *yet*
   > *so*

   e.g., "I went to the store, <u>but</u> I didn't buy anything."

3. Sentence; sentence.
   e.g., "I went to the store; I didn't buy anything."

In the first three rules, sentences are combined by punctuation and the coordinating conjunction.

4. Introductory word or phrase or clause, sentence.
   e.g., of intro word: "I went to the store. <u>However,</u> I didn't buy anything."
   e.g., of intro phrase: "<u>Satisfied with his answers,</u> Joe handed in his test."
   e.g., of intro clause: "<u>Although I went to the store,</u> I didn't buy anything."

5. Sentence, phrase.
   e.g., "Joe handed in his test, <u>relieved that it was finally over.</u>"

6. Items in a series are separated by commas. Unless instructed otherwise, always have one less comma than items.
   e.g., "My favorite colors are black, navy, and gray."

7. Interrupters are enclosed in commas if the interrupters are not essential for the clarity of the sentence.
   e.g., "Kevin, <u>my brother,</u> is a twin."

8. Sentence; word or phrase or list or sentence.
   e.g., of a word: "Tim indicated his anger in one word: <u>darn.</u>"
   e.g., of a phrase: "The newspaper captured the team's motto: 'Grace under pressure.'"
   e.g., of a list: "The following students were elected to office: <u>Sue Green, Joe Blake, and John Jay.</u>"
   e.g., of a sentence: "Greg's father demanded that Greg comply with one rule: <u>Greg was never to break curfew.</u>"

Lesson Plans for Teaching Writing edited by Chris Jennings Dixon © 2007 National Council of Teachers of English.

Figure 5.1

LESSON 53
"BEEF UP YOUR VERBS": USING VIVID LANGUAGE

Wendy C. Kelleher

Purpose

- To develop skills in word choice, especially verb usage

Preparation

Review the Six Traits (ideas, voice, word choice, organization, sentence fluency, and conventions) in Vicki Spandel's *Creating Writers through 6-Trait Writing Assessment and Instruction*, 4th ed., to present the importance of selecting words that convey specific meaning.

Props/Materials

- "Silly Walk" sketch from *Monty Python and the Holy Grail* (Video Collector's Ed., 1975) available at Amazon.com
- *The Day Jimmy's Boa Ate the Wash* by Trinka Hales Noble, illustrated by Steven Kellogg
- My Action Verb List/Beef Up the VERB handout (Figure 5.2)
- A VERY Boring Story/An Exciting and Fun Story handout (Figure 5.3)

Process/Procedure

1. Begin with an attention grabber (anticipatory activity).

> *Teacher:* People don't just go across a room, right? Sometimes they shuffle, sometimes they stride. Sometimes they skip or slouch. What are other ways people move across a room? (Allow time for response.)

> Here are some examples of how people can walk. (Show video of Monty Python's "Silly Walk.")

> *Teacher:* When you write a story, people need descriptive words in order to SEE what is happening because unlike a movie (like the one we just saw), there's no picture except the one you create in the reader's mind. And a story is much more exciting when you can

actually SEE someone doing something. One way to
do that is to use strong verbs, or action words, that are
vivid, like *jump* or *crouch* or *march* or *hop*.

2. Introduce a language product (a literary product from outside the
classroom written by a famous author).

> *Teacher:* I'm going to share a section of a story that shows
> how exciting a story can be when the writer uses vivid
> action words or VERBS. (Read a section of *The Day
> Jimmy's Boa Ate the Wash*.)

3. Guide students in brainstorming/feedback: Freewriting activity with
the entire class.

> *Teacher:* Let's brainstorm. Again, I will write as fast as I
> can while you tell us some of the verbs the author
> used to describe Jimmy's actions when the boa ate his
> mother's wash. (Allow time for feedback.)

4. Distribute My Action Verb List for students to review synonyms for
walk. Divide the class into groups to construct two additional lists of
synonyms using two of the verbs generated from class discussion.

5. Provide directions for writing activity. Detail what steps to follow but
be open to students' creative innovations.

> *Teacher:* Before you write your story like *The Day Jimmy's
> Boa Ate the Wash*, I'm going to share an example of two
> stories I wrote. See if you can tell which story used
> action verbs. (Read A VERY Boring Story handout
> aloud and allow time for students to respond to Story
> 1 and then read Story 2.)

> *Teacher:* Now that we know the difference between a
> boring story and an exciting story, I want you to think
> of a story you could tell about a day like Jimmy had
> when the unexpected happened. Tell the story but use
> exciting verbs to describe the action as you tell us the
> story. Make the story as wild and crazy as you can.
> The more unbelievable, the better!

6. Students begin writing with the teacher during a given time period.

> *Teacher:* Does everyone know what you're going to write
> about? Ready, set, WRITE!

Pointers or Pitfalls

Teaching parts of speech is always seen as boring and lifeless, but this activity can be fun as you act out the different ways people can walk or as you allow students to watch Monty Python's characters. Any story can be used to illustrate the use of action verbs, but my favorite is this Trinka Hales Noble story.

Ponderings

Verbs can be fun!

My Action Verb List

Construct synonyms for each of the following verbs.

Walked	_____	_____
Strode	_____	_____
Ambled	_____	_____
Sprinted	_____	_____
Sashayed	_____	_____
Marched	_____	_____
Goose-stepped	_____	_____
Scissor-kicked	_____	_____
Strolled	_____	_____
Hopped	_____	_____
Limped	_____	_____
Rambled	_____	_____
Wandered	_____	_____
Paraded	_____	_____
Waddled	_____	_____
Tramped	_____	_____
Stomped	_____	_____
Paced	_____	_____
Traveled	_____	_____
Promenaded	_____	_____
Swayed	_____	_____
Swished	_____	_____
Lurched	_____	_____
Shambled	_____	_____
Duck-walked	_____	_____
Trotted	_____	_____
Padded	_____	_____
Waggled	_____	_____
Raced	_____	_____
Ran	_____	_____
Advanced	_____	_____

Beef up the VERB – Review the three sample sentences and rewrite three of your own.

Mrs. Kelleher <u>went</u> across the room. (BLAH!!!!!)
Mrs. Kelleher <u>walked</u> across the room. (Hmmm. OK, but still a little ho-hum)
Mrs. Kelleher <u>sprinted</u> across the room. (Terrific!! I can see that!)

Mrs. Kelleher _____ across the room.

Mrs. Kelleher _____ across the room.

Mrs. Kelleher _____ across the room.

Lesson Plans for Teaching Writing edited by Chris Jennings Dixon © 2007 National Council of Teachers of English.

Figure 5.2

A VERY Boring Story

By Wendy C. Kelleher

A girl <u>went</u> into a room. She <u>sat</u> down. She <u>looked</u> out the window. A boy <u>went</u> into the room. He <u>looked</u> at the girl, then <u>sat</u> next to her. They <u>looked</u> out the window. They <u>talked</u> with each other. Then they <u>saw</u> a friend <u>coming</u> into the same room. The friend <u>said</u>, "Hi, you guys. What <u>are</u> you <u>doing</u>?" They <u>said</u>, "We <u>are looking</u> out of the window. What <u>are</u> you <u>doing</u>?" He said, "I am <u>looking</u> at you." He <u>sat</u> down next to them. They <u>looked</u> out of the window. They <u>were</u> very <u>bored</u>. The girl went out of the room. The boy <u>went</u> out of the room. The other boy <u>went</u> out of the room.

versus

An Exciting and Fun Story

By Wendy C. Kelleher

A girl <u>flounced</u> into a room. She <u>plopped</u> down. She <u>peered</u> out the window. A boy <u>strutted</u> into the room. He <u>leered</u> at the girl, then <u>snuggled</u> next to her. They <u>gazed</u> out the window. They <u>gossiped</u> with each other. Then they <u>glared</u> at a friend <u>sneaking</u> into the same room. The friend <u>blustered</u>, "Hi, you guys. What <u>gives</u>?" They <u>retorted</u>, "We <u>are staring</u> out of the window. What <u>are</u> you <u>plotting</u>?" He <u>snapped</u>, "I am <u>scrutinizing</u> you." He <u>plunked</u> down next to them. They <u>glanced</u> out the window. They <u>sized</u> up each other. The girl <u>slipped</u> out of the room. The boy <u>stomped</u> out of the room. The other boy <u>ambled</u> out of the room.

Figure 5.3

LESSON 54
"DON'T CORRECT—HIGHLIGHT": IDENTIFYING COMMON ERRORS

Sherri Bova

Purpose

- To increase student awareness of common errors in diction, detail, syntax, and grammar

Preparation

Students prepare first or second drafts using prompts provided by the teacher. The teacher then prepares a list of editing goals based on common errors found in student writing or upon class reinforcement of particular writing strategies.

Props/Materials

Yellow, green, blue, and purple highlighters

Process/Procedure

1. Teacher lists editing goals on the blackboard. A highlighter color is assigned for each editing goal. The board may read:
   Goals for today's editing session:

   Develop variety in opening sentences.

   Practice use of vivid verbs.

   Be sure to use specific details for each idea.

   Include transition words to show connections.

   Color Editing Code:

   Blue—Highlight the first word in each sentence

   Yellow—Highlight every use of the "to be" verb

   Green—Highlight all details in body paragraphs

   Purple—Highlight all transition words

2. Students bring their drafts to class and exchange papers.

3. Students are instructed to read the papers and highlight the items as identified on the blackboard. (I allow approximately twenty minutes for this exercise.)

4. Students are instructed to return the papers and discuss the highlighted areas with their peers.

5. Students are assigned to revise their papers to write additional drafts using insights gained from their highlighting activities.

Pointers or Pitfalls

Start off with something simple and work up to more involved editing of common errors. The color coding can be used to emphasize a grammatical structure or a writing stylistic device.

Ponderings

Simple editing assignments work very well with lower level students. I assign more involved items as the year progresses; however, I keep a close watch on the students' responses and back off if the items get too involved.

LESSON 55
HIGHLIGHTING FOR SENTENCE VARIETY: EXPERIMENTING WITH SYNTAX

Suzy S. Bolton

Purpose

- To practice alternative syntax to create various sentence openings

Preparation

To encourage students to experiment with different syntax and to recognize that they can create more fluid prose by becoming conscious of how they begin sentences, discuss the notion that sound can affect a reader's experience of a text and that many writers fall into repeated, unconscious habits. Note that often inexperienced writers will begin all of their sentences with pronouns and/or nouns or the same repeated introductory phrase. Present a student example or prepare a teacher model of a draft that lacks variety in sentence openings and of a revision with varied sentence openings.

Props/Materials

Highlighter; drafts of student compositions, and overhead projector

Process/Procedure

1. Using drafts of compositions that have already been prepared, students highlight the first words in all sentences, ignoring *a*, *and*, and *the*.

2. Students count the number of nouns and pronouns that they used to start sentences.

3. Using teacher prepared transparencies, the teacher presents three or four ways students may alter their openings.

4. Students revise their drafts to create varied sentence openings.

5. Students share their before and after sentences aloud with the class.

Pointers or Pitfalls

This brief example is just that—one way to use highlighters to let students see where they can revise. There are other ways to vary sentence beginnings, for sure. It is important to be specific when demonstrating examples of ways students may alter openings. Three examples that work well are

1. Use a prepositional phrase:
   "At 7 P.M. we left for the airport."
   (instead of) "We left for the airport at 7 P.M."

2. Use two adjectives:
   "Tired and hungry, we waited for the plane to land."
   (instead of) "We were tired and hungry as we waited for the plane to land."

3. Use a participial phrase:
   "Waiting for the plane, we grew tired and hungry."

   (instead of) "We grew tired and hungry as we waited for the plane."

In addition to guiding students to improve sentence openings, I use the highlighters to help students see where they have enough, not enough, or too much support for ideas. (For example, "Highlight specific examples in paragraph 3.") I have even had students highlight each quotation in a research paper to indicate if they have enough, not enough, or too much quoted material. When these very visual students, who were brought up with televisions and video games, can see errors, they can take steps to correct them.

Ponderings

I also use highlighters to show students what I want them to revise. I am a teacher who tries to get students to reduce use of *to be* verbs and to use more vivid verbs. If I am reading a draft, I keep a highlighter handy. When I return a draft with ten to fifteen uses of *to be* highlighted on one page, the student is astounded. "I had no idea I had used that verb so often!" is a common reaction. Of course, students are equally delighted that they do not have to rewrite all of their sentences, just some of them. Highlighters can be an effective way to locate very l-o-n-g sentences, and they are very effective in revealing fragments or run-ons. I think the key in revision is to give a student a focused, specific task. Then the revision becomes user-friendly, and the writing improves.

LESSON 56
GRIEVOUS GRAMMAR ERRORS:
PROOFREADING FOR COMMON ERRORS

Christopher Smutzer

Purpose

- To proofread composition drafts in order to correct errors in sentence fragments, run-ons, comma splices, grammatically misspelled words, and pronoun-antecedent reference.

Preparation

Before this activity, provide lessons and practice in correct use of grammar rules for six areas: (1) sentence fragments, (2) run-ons, (3) subject-verb agreement, (4) comma splices, (5) grammatically misspelled words, and (6) pronoun-antecedent.

Props/Materials

Overhead transparency; overhead projector

Process/Procedure

1. Teacher collects a set of papers and identifies examples of sentences containing problems in any of the six areas of grammar studied.

2. The teacher types each of the examples and makes a transparency of the errors, usually about ten to fifteen sentences. Title this transparency "Grievous Grammar Errors."

3. The class reviews the transparency of anonymous sentences.

4. As a class, students identify types of errors and offer suggestions to remedy each sentence.

5. The teacher revises each sentence using student feedback.

6. Following this whole class review of weak sentences, the original set of papers is returned to the students.

7. Students revise their papers with special attention to the six grammatical rules.

Pointers or Pitfalls

I do not tell who made what errors on the excerpted sentences, but most of the time, students volunteer that they wrote that really long run-on or silly fragment. Students are not used to seeing their errors in isolation like this and seeing them in isolation from their papers seems to make them better proofreaders.

Ponderings

Teaching grammar using the students' own sentences is much better than giving them those dry grammar activities from their grammar or writing handbooks.

LESSON 57
GRAPHING SENTENCES: DEVELOPING STYLE

Christopher Smutzer

Purpose

- To vary sentence beginnings and structures to develop a more sophisticated style

Preparation

The teacher assigns students to write a first draft related to a topic of class studies. The teacher may also need to review x- and y-axis points on a graph.

Props/Materials

Graph paper, drafts of student composition

Process/Procedure

1. Using graph paper, students create grids for each of the sentences in their drafts.

2. Students write the first word of each sentence from a given paragraph horizontally using the x-axis on the graph paper.

3. The teacher directs students to identify repetitions in their first words.

4. Then students count the number of words in each sentence of their paragraphs and convey the sentence length numbers (one for each sentence) to their graphs vertically using the y-axis.

5. Students connect the dots along the y-axis to see if their sentence lengths in their paragraphs "zigzag" or "flatline" on the graph.

6. The teacher provides suggestions and examples of variety for creating improved sentence openings.

7. Students return to their original drafts to revise for variety in sentence lengths and sentence openings.

Pointers or Pitfalls

I tell my students that the graph for each of their paragraphs should ideally look like a *W* or an *M*. This means that the sentences vary in length. This activity can be done with all levels of students. At first, though, you may want to have students only write and graph one paragraph instead of an entire essay.

Ponderings

I am constantly telling my upper-level students that they must adopt a more sophisticated writing style. This activity provides one way to point them in that direction. It makes students aware of word choice and types of sentences.

LESSON 58
ERROR ANALYSIS PATTERNS: PROMOTING SELF-ASSESSMENT STRATEGIES

Chris Jennings Dixon

Purpose

- To increase sensitivity to Standard Written English
- To identify and review common errors in written composition
- To diagnose individual areas of concern in sentence structure, usage, capitalization, and punctuation

Preparation

With a solid base of exposure to and practice in basic mechanics of composition, students can identify and review their own individual weaknesses. Approaching error analysis from an inductive or a deductive mode can be handled in two warm-up activities after students have written their drafts.

  1. The teacher reads student papers and identifies at least one type of error in each category of the Areas of Concern chart. These errors are presented to the students on

a handout. Using the chart, students review the items in an open class discussion or in groups, use their writing handbooks to pose grammatical explanations, and suggest various ways to remedy each type of error.

2. Students are asked to bring professional examples of well-written essays from a book or magazine or newspaper article. In group discussions, students share their articles and make a list of fifteen characteristics in the areas of sentence structure, usage, capitalization, and punctuation that make the essays effective and well written. The teacher then compiles a class summary. Students review the summary and the Areas of Concern chart to determine common writing traits.

Props/Materials

Areas of Concern chart (Figure 5.4)
Writing handbook

Process/Procedure

1. After the warm-up activity, teacher distributes Areas of Concern chart to students to place in their writing folders.

2. Following each writing assignment, students receive feedback through teacher review, peer review, or self-assessment related to aspects covered on the charts.

3. Students review feedback and use their writing handbooks to identify patterns of errors and remedies.

4. Each student identifies his or her major areas that need improvement based upon preceding compositions.

5. Each student lists the top three items as a focus for drafting and revision in a subsequent writing assignment. (This list may be written at the top of the next draft as a reminder.)

6. Students continuously review ways to remedy their errors and demonstrate an understanding of their rationale through reflective assignments, such as "In this paper, I concentrated on _____ because _____."

7. Students maintain records of their areas of concern on their charts to regularly review progress.

8. The teacher can use data from student charts to prepare mini-lessons to provide help with common or ongoing problems in writing.

Pointers or Pitfalls

Because a preponderance of errors can be overwhelming to students, teacher feedback needs to be encouraging, noting improvements along the way. Students need to realize they are learning to control their written expression through recognition of patterns of errors and "corrections." The teacher needs to take time to encourage and praise efforts of students to handle their own assessment and revision strategies.

Ponderings

Using error analysis can be time consuming in the first stages; however, once students take charge of their own checklists, the process enables them to better understand Standard Written English. As they become empowered in analyzing their writing, they develop more sophistication in their language skills.

Areas of Concern			
Paper Title:			
Sentence Structure	Comma Splice (CS)			
	Run-On Sentence (RO)			
	Sentence Fragment (SF)			
Usage Errors	Subject-Verb Agreement (SV)			
	Verb Tense Shift (VT)			
	Pronoun Problems (Pro)			
	Punctuation [commas, apostrophes, quotes] (P)			
	Organizational Problems (O)			

Lesson Plans for Teaching Writing edited by Chris Jennings Dixon © 2007
National Council of Teachers of English.

Figure 5.4

LESSON 59
SIGNPOSTS TO MEANING:
UNDERSTANDING PUNCTUATION

Michele Marits

Purpose

- To identify how punctuation affects meaning
- To demonstrate understanding of the relationship between grammar and punctuation

Preparation

Review capitalization and punctuation usage with the class.

Props/Materials

Writing handbook

Process/Procedure

1. The teacher asks students to select two sentences from a published text to bring to class. These sentences may come from fiction or nonfiction sources.

2. Students read the two sentences from the published text to write an explanation of capitalization and the punctuation (periods, commas, hyphens, semicolons, quotation marks, etc.) that the writer used.

3. Students may refer to a writing handbook or ask the teacher for assistance.

4. Finally, students type or handwrite their explanations, the author's name, and title of the source on a sheet of paper to submit at the end of the dictation activity.

5. The teacher instructs the students to do the following:

   In class, s-l-o-w-l-y read the text aloud to your small group or to the entire class. While you are reading your dictation, your group members handwrite on paper or type on a computer screen what you are dictating. Listeners are to capitalize and insert punctuation marks they think the writer used in the sentences.

6. Students take turns as dictators and scribers to re-create selected sentences.

7. When the class or small group finishes writing and punctuating the dictated sentences, student listeners-scribers share their versions of the original sentences.

8. Students compare capitalization and punctuation in the original text to their dictated versions.

9. Students explain why the writers of their selected sentences use certain punctuation marks. Students need to be able to justify their explanations with references to a writing handbook.

10. The teacher guides a discussion of how punctuation is used by authors to convey meaning.

Pointers or Pitfalls

By explaining a writer's punctuation and by listening to the reasons writers use certain punctuation marks, students gain a better understanding of grammar. Teachers should model this activity for the students to help them understand the entire process.

Ponderings

Although this activity originated from a graduate teaching course, it is adaptable for any level.

LESSON 60
THE "LOOK": FORMATTING PARAGRAPHS

Marty Brooks

Purpose

- To develop awareness and practice in formatting paragraphs for visual effect

Preparation

To demonstrate that while paragraphing is used to let the reader know that the writer is shifting from one point or event to another, paragraphing also has a visual dimension and that the "look" of a paragraph has an effect on the reader. This exercise raises the idea that writers' paragraphs change depending on the medium in which they are writing. Choose a long newspaper article; then type out a section of that newspaper article without paragraph breaks. Be sure to single space and use a small font (9- or 10-point) when typing the section. Fill half to two-thirds of a standard page to encourage students to create longer paragraphs when you ask them to insert their own paragraph breaks.

Props/Materials

- Excerpted newspaper article (teacher prepared)
- Original newspaper article
- Entire section of newspaper, if available

Process/Procedure

1. Teacher distributes copies of the excerpted and reformatted article.

2. Each student inserts a *P* in the excerpted article to indicate where he or she would make paragraph breaks.

3. After all students have done this, the teacher goes to the blackboard and asks students to relate the number of paragraphs identified. (Usually, the number varies between three and eight.)

4. The teacher should also ask students to identify where the breaks occur. (Usually, the places where students make breaks overlap.)

5. Then, referring to the original article, students make slashes where the original writer of the article has made paragraph breaks. (Since the text is from a newspaper article, it probably has paragraph breaks for every one or two sentences.)

6. The teacher leads a discussion of why the writer has made so many paragraph breaks.

7. Finally, the teacher leads the class to discuss the variability of paragraphing, the fact that paragraphing responds

to readers' visual needs, and the different effects of different lengths of paragraphs. This last point is best made by asking the students to imagine what they would do if they encountered a newspaper article in which the first paragraph was eight or nine inches in length.

Pointers or Pitfalls

Be sure to note that the point in this exercise is not that students write one or two sentence paragraphs. In the format in which they are usually working, such paragraphing looks choppy and is distracting. However, students need to be aware of how paragraph variety creates a visual impact.

Ponderings

This exercise is very helpful for students who develop their ideas but create so many paragraph breaks that their papers seem disjointed. It is also helpful for those students who do not develop their points. You can tell them that they can not just combine their choppy paragraphing like a newspaper article. Rather they need to add more detail. Finally, this exercise shows students that they do have some text savvy as they compare reader expectations and paragraph formatting techniques.

VI Writing on Demand

"Are we teaching to the test?" echoes across classrooms in the United States in response to national-, state-, and district-mandated evaluations of student achievement in writing. Despite pedagogical approaches to teaching writing as a process and academic recognition that measurement of authentic writing practices is the preferable assessment mode, the common approach to gathering evidence of student achievement in composition continues to be conducted in the most efficient, economic manner, usually via short, often timed, writing samples. Additionally, in the interest of expediency, college and university composition programs employ writing samples to identify entering students who need remediation to succeed in college writing programs. To expose students to this approach and provide practice in this genre, teacher-contributors in this section present activities for student mastery of writing on demand for varied venues.

LESSON 61
MUSIC IN THE CLASSROOM: JOURNALING FOR TIMED WRITINGS

Dorothy K. Fletcher

Purpose

- To practice timed writings using music as a catalyst for discussion

Preparation

Because recent brain research finds that playing soft instrumental music while "creating" enhances the creative product, I play such music while students write in journals for timed writings. At the beginning of the year, I briefly explain that this activity will happen twice a week for the rest of the year, and I talk about the brain research that supports this activity. "The Quotations Page" is a good resource for familiar quotes to use as writing prompts.

Props/Materials

- Student composition book (kept in a file drawer in classroom)
- Four to five CDs of jazz, relaxation, or movie sound tracks
- "The Quotations Page" at www.quotationspage.com/

Process/Procedure

Using instrumental music, students write in their journals (composition books) for thirty minutes twice a week. The teacher provides familiar quotations that students analyze as a class. Using a selected quotation, students are instructed that their first paragraphs must explain the literal meaning of the quotation. Subsequent paragraphs must provide real-life examples and illustrations of this quotation in action. Students are required to write a minimum of three hundred words at each sitting.

Pointers or Pitfalls

Initially, some students may complain that writing three hundred words is too much. Often they are surprised by the length of their responses once they get started. Other students may want to talk during the music, breaking the concentration of their neighbors. The teacher needs to remind students not to talk while the music is playing as the talking will not only distract others but make their brain circuits travel to their less creative left hemispheres. Usually a gentle reminder can get everyone back on track.

Ponderings

I find that after the students have done this procedure for several sessions, their writing becomes far more "fluid." Students can also use this session as a contemplative time—one that is peaceful and calm. The "angst" level in general seems to be lower when I use this activity consistently. The overall quality of the student writing seems better because students seem to be able to support their conclusions with details, and they can also fill their work with more vivid details because they have been forced to meet a three hundred-word requirement.

LESSON 62
"WHY WRITE?" PRACTICING RESPONSE WRITING

Sue Buck

Purpose

- To articulate the purpose for writing from a personal perspective compared to the professional writer's view
- To practice response writing for journal entries

Preparation

Advanced preparation to answer "Why write?" in journal; one week prior to the assignment, discuss reasons for writing in a journal.

Props/Materials

"Why Write?" Reflections on the Art of Writing handout (with quotations) (Figure 6.1)
Student journals

Process/Procedure

1. Students write a response in their journals to the question "Why write?"

2. One week later, the teacher distributes Reflections on the Art of Writing handouts and instructs students to review quotations by professional writers about the importance of writing.

3. Each student selects a quotation by a writer that seems to speak to him or her.

4. In their journals, students respond to their selected quotations in short responses over a timed period of approximately fifteen minutes.

5. The teacher leads follow-up discussions soliciting students to share their written responses. Thus, classmates develop a greater appreciation for and an understanding of the writing process.

Pointers or Pitfalls

Do not let students see the quotations about writing until they have written their first entry in response to "Why write?"

Ponderings

Since student samples provide better insight into the reflection process for this type of writing, save samples, with permission, from past students to share with the class.

"Why Write?" Reflections on the Art of Writing

1. Read what some people have written about the importance of writing.

2. Do any of the quotations mirror your philosophy or say something similar to what you wrote in your journal?

"We . . . write to heighten our own awareness of life. . . . We write to taste life twice, in the moment and in retrospection. . . . We write to be able to transcend our life, to reach beyond it . . . to teach ourselves to speak with others, to record the journey into the labyrinth . . . to expand our world, when we feel strangled, constricted, lonely. . . . When I don't write, I feel my world shrinking. I feel I lose my fire, my color." —Anaïs Nin

"A writer needs three things, experience, observation, and imagination, any two of which, at times any one of which, can supply the lack of the others." —William Faulkner

"Writing is nothing more than a guided dream." —Jorge Luis Borges

"Writing is easy. All you do is stare at a blank sheet of paper until drops of blood form on your forehead." —Gene Fowler

"Talking is a hydrant in the yard and writing is a faucet upstairs in the house. Opening the first takes all the pressure off the second." —Robert Frost

"There are only two powers in the world, the sword and the pen, and in the end the former is always conquered by the latter." —Napoleon

"The two most engaging powers of an author are, to make new things familiar, and familiar things new." —Samuel Johnson

"Talent alone cannot make a writer. There must be a man behind the book." —Ralph Waldo Emerson

"Writing has laws of perspectives, of light, and shade, just as painting does, or music. If you are born knowing them, fine. If not, learn them. Then rearrange the rules to suit yourself." —Truman Capote

"Thought Flies and words go on foot. Therein lies all the drama of a writer." —Julien Green

"True ease in writing comes from art, not chance. As those move easiest when they have learned to dance." —Alexander Pope

"There is no royal path to good writing; and such paths as exist do not lead through neat critical gardens, various as they are, but through the jungles of self, the world, and of craft." —Jessamyn West

continued on next page

Figure 6.1

Figure 6.1 continued

"A writer is essentially a man who does not resign himself to loneliness."
—Francois Mauriac

"In a very real sense, the writer writes in order to teach himself to understand himself, to satisfy himself; the publishing of his ideas, though it brings gratifications, is a curious anticlimax." —Alfred Kazin

"From writing rapidly it does not result that one writes well, but from writing well it results that one writes rapidly." —Quintilian

"A writer lives at best in a state of astonishment. Beneath any feeling he has of the good or evil of the world lies a deeper one of wonder at it all. To transmit that feeling, he writes." —William Sansom

"Most people won't realize that writing is a craft. You have to take your apprenticeship in it like anything else." —Katherine Anne Porter

"There is no lighter burden, nor more agreeable, than a pen." —Petrarch

"The writer is the Faust of modern society, the only surviving individualist in a mass age. To his orthodox contemporaries, he seems semi-madman." —Boris Pasternak

"The next thing most like living one's life over again seems to be a recollection of that life, and to make that recollection as durable as possible by putting it in writing." —Benjamin Franklin

"Of all those arts which the wise excel,/Nature's chief masterpiece is writing well." —John Sheffield

"The great poet, in writing himself, writes his time." —T. S. Eliot

"The pen is the tongue of the mind." —Cervantes

"Reading maketh a full man, conference a ready man, and writing an exact man." —Francis Bacon

"A poem, a sentence, causes us to see ourselves. I be, and I see my being, at the same time." —Ralph Waldo Emerson

"The writer and nothing else: a man alone in a room with the English language, trying to get human feelings right." —John K. Hutchens

LESSON 63
QUOTING *MACBETH*: AN IN-CLASS TIMED WRITING

Dale DeSarro

Purpose

- To practice writing in a timed mode
- To analyze symbolic language in a literary work

Preparation

Students need to have read and studied Shakespeare's *Macbeth*.

Props/Materials

- *Macbeth* by William Shakespeare
- Any notes the students may have taken from classroom discussions
- In-Class Timed Writing Assignment and Grading Scale handout (Figure 6.2)

Process/Procedure

1. The teacher distributes the In-class Timed Writing Assignment and Grading Scale handout.

2. In class, students write their essays on the symbolic word using only the text and any notes they have already taken from class discussions.

3. The teacher stresses that students may not exceed the time limit and should use their time wisely. (The individual teacher can determine the amount of time based on the results being sought. Forty-five minutes to an hour seems to be a fair amount of time, but since the point is to get students to write within a certain amount of time, set a limit and stick to it. Use a timer if necessary.)

4. In-class timed essays may be scored by three other students using the grading scale on the handout. (Scoring sheets should be prepared for each reader to use.)

Pointers or Pitfalls

Students who are absent on the day the prep sheet is distributed pose a problem. Distributing the sheet a couple of days before the "in-class" part, so everyone knows ahead of time, seems to help. Students who do miss either the prep sheet or the "in-class" portion should be aware that they need to make up the activities on their own time, just like a test. Since forty-five minutes to an hour is a long time for high school students to give up outside of class, they seem to be more stimulated to be in class and prepared.

Ponderings

Students respond well to the opportunity to prepare for a testlike essay, and the results are better and more thoughtful than regular essay questions on a test. This activity is also a great way to show students what they are required to do on later essay tests/exams and in college.

In-Class Timed Writing Assignment

Each of the following quotations contains an underlined word. Using your book and any notes that you may have taken during this class period ONLY, choose *one* of the words and write a well-thought-out essay explaining the significance and use of this word THROUGHOUT THE PLAY. Proofread your work carefully and thoroughly and watch the time.

"Sleep no more! Macbeth does murder sleep."

"What, will these hands ne'er be clean?"

"The night is long that never finds the day."

"Blood will have blood."

- -

Grading Scale for In-Class Timed Writing Assignment

Writer: _____   Peer Reader:_____

_____ Traces word throughout the play

_____ Legible

_____ Proofread for mechanics

_____ Well thought out

_____ Obviously researched (or paid close attention in class)

Lesson Plans for Teaching Writing edited by Chris Jennings Dixon © 2007 National Council of Teachers of English.

Figure 6.2

LESSON 64
NEWSPAPERS AND MAGAZINES: USING HEADLINES AS PROMPTS

Susan P. Allen

Purpose

- To draft, write, and revise a composition within a timed class period

Preparation

Collect newspapers and magazines

Props/Materials

- Newspapers
- Magazines

Process/Procedure:

1. Students spend about ten minutes skimming newspapers and magazines, looking for recurrent themes or topics in the headlines (crime, natural disaster, environmental concerns, specific political issues, etc.).

2. Students write down the topics and/or themes on sheets of paper.

3. Each student selects one topic or theme of interest.

4. Students spend the remainder of the class period writing in response to the following prompts (Thirty to forty minutes):

    - Explain why you believe the theme or topic you have identified is interesting to readers

    - Relate what this topic or theme may suggest about human nature

    - Explain the implications of this topic or theme for society.

Pointers or Pitfalls

Finding space to store periodicals may be difficult, especially for "traveling" teachers. Students can be assigned to bring in magazines and newspapers for class use on designated days. Another avenue for resources is the Internet. If possible, the teacher can arrange for students to meet in a computer lab where they can more easily access past and current newspaper and magazine headlines.

Ponderings

Providing current literature seems to motivate students to write on topics with which they are familiar in a short, timed period.

LESSON 65
COLLEGE EXPECTATIONS: IMPROMPTU IN-CLASS ESSAY

Stuart D. Noel

Purpose

- To practice writing an essay to prepare for the Regent's Essay Exam (a requirement of the State of Georgia) or for other regionally mandating assessments

Preparation

Teacher-led discussion, student practice, and feedback in writing essays

Props/Materials

Georgia Perimeter College English Exit Examination/Writing Sample (Figure 6.3)

Process/Procedure

At unannounced times, students are asked to choose one of three topics on which to compose their writing samples. These activities are timed. The teacher needs to recreate the testing conditions of an English exit examination as closely as possible. Administering the Georgia Perimeter College English Exit Examination/Writing Sample provides motivated practice for composing in this mode. If possible, outside raters need to be found, student writing samples should be sent for assessment outside of the classroom, and the results of these assessments should be shared with students.

Pointers or Pitfalls

The activity can be used to stimulate discussion between high school and college faculties. Additionally, it aids students in discovering what colleges are looking for in college composition.

Ponderings

From my work with college and high school teachers, I have found that preparation for college is a major factor in the high school teacher's day-to-day goals; thus, the writing assessment presents an opportunity for students to become comfortable with a bonafide institutional practice. This activity also provides essential practice for students in their high school years who may not be planning to go to college but later find themselves registering and having to demonstrate writing proficiency in short writing samples like this sample exit examination.

Georgia Perimeter College English Exit Examination/Writing Sample (90 minutes)

General Directions

Choose one of the three topics below and write a well-organized essay within the allotted time. The acceptable essay will require that you (1) state and develop a thesis (central idea); (2) organize to show an overall plan; (3) deal with the assigned topic; (4) avoid serious errors in grammar, diction, sentence structure, and paragraph development. Your paper will be read and evaluated by multiple raters. They will not know your identity. A passing writing sample requires the agreement of two raters.

Specific Directions

1. Write at least a four-paragraph essay on the chosen topic. <u>You must write on one of the topics listed</u>. Be sure to include an introductory paragraph, at least two body paragraphs, and a concluding paragraph in your paper.

2. Write legibly; <u>raters must be able to read your essay</u>

3. Write the essay in ink (required) on every other line of the blue book or type the essay using a computer (CAI classes only). Suggested time frame:

   –ten minutes to choose the topic and plan the essay.

   –ten minutes to write the introduction

   –fifty minutes to write the support paragraphs and the conclusion

   –twenty minutes to proofread and edit

4. Organize on the back of this page.

5. Use your dictionary during the last fifteen minutes <u>only</u>.

6. Put an **X** in the blank next to the chosen topic.

   _____ What would you do if you won the lottery?

   _____ Should elementary school students be required to wear uniforms? Why or why not?

   _____ What foreign country would you like to visit, and why would you like to go there?

Writing Sample ____ SOCIAL SECURITY # _____ Posting Code _____

Lesson Plans for Teaching Writing edited by Chris Jennings Dixon © 2007 National Council of Teachers of English.

Figure 6.3

LESSON 66
ORIENTATION TO COLLEGE: CREATING A WRITING SAMPLE

Chris Jennings Dixon

Purpose

- To experience the college day and be acquainted with college resources
- To practice a writing mode often used to assess student readiness for college writing
- To develop an understanding of the requirements for college admission

Preparation

Students should be polled to determine interest in visiting a nearby college. College personnel in the areas of administration, counseling, admissions, testing, and library resources need to be contacted to establish a schedule for visitations. College faculty and college students need to be solicited to facilitate high school student visits and interviews about college academic and social life. High school students need to be aware that they have an opportunity to engage in an assessment of their readiness for college work. Field trip forms need to be prepared and completed. Bus transportation needs to be reserved and funded. Teacher/parent chaperones need to be identified. Funding for refreshments needs to be secured. Class lists of student visitors need to be prepared in advance for planning purposes.

Props/Materials

- Activity Schedule for High School Field Trips handout for all participants (Figure 6.4)
- Welcome packets and admissions materials as available from the college
- Library Use for Outside Patrons materials as available from the college
- Writing Sample Instructions (Figure 6.5)

Process/Procedure:

1. Students travel from their high school to the college with teacher/parent chaperones and follow an activity schedule as developed by all participants.

2. At the college, students are ushered to a common meeting site where they are welcomed by the administration, receive welcome packets, and are treated to refreshments.

3. Students are divided into groups to tour various parts of the campus and meet with appropriate college personnel.

4. College students working as orientation guides respond to student questions during the tour.

5. As students visit the library/media center and interact with resource personnel and resources, they may have an opportunity to complete information to obtain a college/community library card.

6. Students may have an opportunity to visit a college class in session.

7. Students may have an opportunity to visit the admissions office to receive information about requirements for admission and registration.

8. At the college placement center, students may take a twenty-minute paragraph writing test to assist in determining their composition placement (see Writing Sample Instructions handout).

9. Writing samples can then be sent to college faculty reviewers to determine student readiness for college composition.

10. After students have completed the tour and testing, they may return to a common site for refreshments to discuss their findings with college personnel. Additionally, students can interview guest professors and college students in an informal setting.

11. Following a summation of the day's tour, students then depart via buses to return to their school.

12. Results of the writing assessment tests are gathered and sent to the high school teacher and students with additional information about registering for college classes.

Pointers or Pitfalls

This field trip activity usually takes a half day of school; however, since many seniors leave school early for employment, they miss an entire school day. Most students miss their lunch time, thus, the need to provide refreshments.

Students are often surprised by the results of the writing assessment tests and teachers discover the value of an outside evaluator to motivate their students to improve their skills. If students are to be tested using placement materials at the college, they need to be divided into groups that can efficiently be handled by the testing facilities. If the writing assessment allows students to complete the work at their own pace, arrangements need to be made to accommodate these variations.

It is vital that a workable schedule be created that allows sufficient travel time, interactive dialogue, touring, and testing.

Ponderings

Students, teachers, and parent chaperones are often surprised to discover the range of offerings by the local college. Students have visited during the fall and spring semesters with equal success. However, the timing of the visits has been a point of concern since students do have different outlooks on attending college at the beginning of their senior year than closer to graduation. To ensure that high school students are prepared for college-level composition, it is preferable to schedule the assessment portion of this activity at the beginning of the school year in order to plan and implement remedial strategies as needed throughout the year.

Activity Schedule for High School Field Trips			
School buses go to college bus stop.			
9:30 – 9:55 A.M.	Welcome and Refreshments—Cafeteria Annex Welcome Remarks:		
	Campus Tour *Counseling/ Admissions*	*Library Orientation*	*Testing Facility*
10:00 – 10:25 A.M.	**GROUP A**	**GROUP B**	**GROUP C**
10:30 – 10:55 A.M.	**GROUP B**	**GROUP C**	**GROUP A**
11:00 – 11:25 A.M.	**GROUP C**	**GROUP A**	**GROUP B**
11:30 – 11:45 A.M.	*All Return to Cafeteria Annex for Refreshments and Discussion*		
11:45 A.M.	*Depart for Bus*		

Lesson Plans for Teaching Writing edited by Chris Jennings Dixon © 2007 National Council of Teachers of English.

Figure 6.4

Writing Sample Instructions	
NAME:	S.S.#
CAMPUS:	DATE:
Is English your native language?	
If not, how many years have you studied English?	
What other languages are spoken in your household?	

For the writing sample, select one of the topics listed below and write an organized, coherent paragraph of approximately 150 words on that subject. For example, if your topic is "driving a car," a topic sentence might be "Driving a car is a hazardous activity." You then give supporting details of how or why driving can be dangerous. Your paragraph should

> 1. Include a topic sentence with **one, clearly stated opinion**
>
> 2. Provide specific examples and details that support that opinion
>
> 3. Be written in grammatically correct, standard English—no lists or outlines

Be sure to proofread your paragraph.

USE AN INK PEN.

You will be allowed twenty minutes to complete the writing sample.

TOPICS: Choose <u>One</u>

        A. Television advertising

        B. Setting goals

        C. Feeling responsible

        D. Ideal partner/mate

        E. Life fifty years from now

Lesson Plans for Teaching Writing edited by Chris Jennings Dixon © 2007 National Council of Teachers of English.

Figure 6.5

VII Media

The Medium Is the Massage (1967) by Marshall McLuhan continues to reverberate in our classrooms today. Any study of language arts would be remiss if it did not include opportunities for students to identify and analyze the power of media and technology on mass communication. The strategies in this section incorporate writing response and critical analysis skills in media-related themes. Through a study of media and its impact on the audience, students learn how media can shape the message. Furthermore, through interactive activities, students gain expertise as consumers of media and develop skills in argumentation. The varied context of these activities enables teachers to promote critical literacy and make real connections with diverse students.

LESSON 67
MEDIA AND WEIGHT LOSS: DEVELOPING AN ARGUMENTATIVE ESSAY

Mary Kay Crouch

Purpose

- To look in-depth at messages in print and broadcast advertising
- To analyze text, layout, visuals, intended audience, and point of view
- To write an argumentative essay discussing the role of advertising in promoting positive messages
- To practice peer readings for revision

Preparation

To teach analysis by using the media, instruct students to look for the idea of "beauty" in magazines that they regularly read. Students need to know ahead of time that they are responsible for bringing in at least one magazine and for choosing one ad they want to discuss. The teacher may also prepare video recordings of ads that appear on TV to augment the discussion.

Props/Materials

- Magazines, videos
- Peer Group Brainstorming handout (Figure 7.1)
- Peer Group Evaluation handout (Figure 7.2)

Process/Procedure:

1. The teacher distributes Peer Group Brainstorming handouts to students.
2. Students respond to questions in their journals and discuss their responses in small peer groups. This preparation eliminates off-the-cuff comments. (See Journal section in Figure 7.1.)

3. With ads that students have brought to class on the topic of "beauty," each group discusses features as suggested in Part B of the handout, although students can go beyond these items.

4. Comments are again written down for presentation to the class as a whole.

5. Finally, other prompts for analyzing the ads are used (see Part C) for students to analyze, not just describe, the ads.

6. From these kinds of prewriting experiences, students begin to form ideas for their own essays based on the positive role the media play in diet and body image.

7. Students use their journal materials to write essays about one segment of media and how this particular segment promotes a positive message.

8. The students prepare their argumentative essays to meet writing standards for focus, development, and organization.

9. The teacher divides the class into groups of three to four students and distributes Peer Group Evaluation handouts. Students submit their essay drafts to their peer groups.

10. Peer readers complete items on the handouts to respond to student drafts.

11. Student writers use peer suggestions to revise and rewrite their essays prior to submitting them to the teacher for assessment.

Pointers or Pitfalls

Students can easily get off-track in their group discussion as well as in their essays because they tend to want to describe rather than analyze. Part B asks students to describe, but Part C takes them beyond simple description to analysis.

Ponderings

Many of the essays will contain more description than analysis, so the teacher needs to help students see the difference between the two approaches.

**Peer Group Brainstorming for Analysis Essay
The Media and Weight Loss Products**

Journal

Before we begin to evaluate magazine ads for weight loss products, please spend about fifteen minutes writing about ads on TV or in magazines, which you recall, that make claims to help people lose weight. Have you ever tried these products? Do you think they work (whether you've tried them or not)? You might also want to consider the following questions:

Why do you think Americans are so concerned about losing weight? Do you have a friend who has tried to lose weight? Was she or he successful? Why do you think she or he was or wasn't?

Peer Group Discussion

Please select one person in your group to take notes on your discussion. That person can also be responsible for reporting to the whole class, or you can choose someone else to read the notes the secretary takes. Because this is a group effort, be sure you indicate who contributed what to the discussion in your group.

A. Begin by discussing in your groups what each person wrote about in the journal, and report your findings to the class when your instructor calls on your group.

B. Please bring in advertisements or articles about weight loss and weight loss products or services, which appear in the magazines you read. Again, take notes on the discussion. As a group, look at and talk about features such as

- the text you find in the ad

- the layout of the ad

- the visuals used

- the intended audience

C. Using the magazines you've brought in, identify the types of people who are represented in the pictures and advertisements. Take notes and share these findings with the class.

- Who are the "beautiful people" that you see most frequently in these magazines?

- Who do you consider to be the five most beautiful people you know or have seen in your life? Do they match those images in the magazines?

Figure 7.1

Figure 7.1 continued

- What is the idea of beauty that the pictures portray?
- How much of a role does weight play in the ideal of beauty shown in the magazines?

Writing Assignment

We have been talking about the negative role that magazines and other media have on diet and body image. For this assignment, I want you to think about the *positive* role the media can play on healthy diet and body image. You can examine advertising, both printed and visual, television, movies, and the Internet to determine how much the media educates and encourages the public to take care of their bodies.

Then prepare to write an essay in which you select only *one* segment of the media (talk shows like *Oprah* or *Ellen*) and discuss the ways in which these shows, ads, and so on, play a positive role in health and body image education. Be sure to make a strong argument for the positive aspects of the media you are studying.

Lesson Plans for Teaching Writing edited by Chris Jennings Dixon © 2007 National Council of Teachers of English.

Peer Group Evaluation
Argument

Writer:

Readers:

Focus: What argument does the writer make that shows the positive role of the media on diet and body image? Write that argument here:

(Writer: If the readers' responses to this question do not reflect your intent, ask the group where you went wrong.)

How well does the writer stay on topic? Can you suggest where she or he should eliminate some details to stay on topic?

Development: What kind of information does the writer give you so that you can understand the ideas presented in the paper? List this information:

What other information, which doesn't appear in the draft, do you need to understand the argument?

Organization: Where can the writer strengthen the organization to make the paper clearer?

Final Feedback: What has the writer done well in this paper? What impressed you when you read this draft?

Lesson Plans for Teaching Writing edited by Chris Jennings Dixon © 2007 National Council of Teachers of English.

Figure 7.2

LESSON 68
PRINT ADVERTISEMENT: WRITING AN ARGUMENTATIVE ESSAY

Susan P. Allen

Purpose

- To write an effective argument analyzing a print advertisement

Preparation

Prepare a mini-lesson on the use of logic in argumentative writing with special emphasis on inductive reasoning, deductive reasoning, emotional appeals, and fallacies.

Props/Materials

- Writing handbook
- Writing an Argument Based on a Print Advertisement handout (Figure 7.3)

Process/Procedure

1. Students are asked to individually select three print ads that are appropriate for class discussions (newspaper, magazine, special flyers) and bring those to class.

2. The teacher guides a discussion on problems in logic that may be found in advertising by modeling an analysis of a common advertisement, such as an ad for an SUV that suggests the vehicle is rugged enough to climb into crevices of the Moon.

3. Using a writing handbook, students review terms such as *inductive reasoning*, *deductive reasoning*, *stereotyping*, *emotional appeals*, and *fallacies*.

4. The teacher distributes Writing an Argument Based on a Print Advertisement handout describing the assignment.

5. Students work in groups of three or four, discussing the ads they brought to class and identifying targeted audience, images, words, colors, etc.

6. Students are instructed to record their brainstorming comments.

7. Each student selects an advertisement to write an outline analyzing the effectiveness or ineffectiveness of the advertisement.

8. From the outlines, students write final drafts of their papers.

Pointers or Pitfalls

Be sure to advise students to select advertisements that are appropriate for classroom discussion.

Ponderings

This is an effective way to guide students as consumers as well as help them to develop their persuasive writing skills. To motivate students, a grade needs to be assigned for the final product.

Writing an Argument Based on a Print Advertisement

What am I supposed to do?

Write a four-hundred to five-hundred word argument. You must analyze a magazine advertisement to determine why it is or is not effective. The analysis should consider the emotional/persuasive appeals discussed in class and the text. The following questions may help you determine what you will include in your essay:

> Is the ad effective? Why or why not?
>
> What is the ad's predominant focus?
>
> Is the product appealing to the consumer's emotional need? How?
>
> What effects do the colors in the ads have? Why?
>
> What effects do objects in the ad have? Why?
>
> What effects do the people and/or animals in the ad have? Why?
>
> Does the ad play on stereotypes? How?
>
> Does the ad make assumptions? What?
>
> To whom is the ad directed? Why do you think so?
>
> Are there any moral issues presented in the ad? What?

Can I select the ad? Yes. The only constraint is that you use ads appropriate for class discussion.

Do I need to submit an outline for this paper? Yes.

How should I submit this assignment?

> Outline with appropriate heading
>
> Advertisement
>
> Final draft of your paper
>
> Rough draft or at least one page of brainstorming

Lesson Plans for Teaching Writing edited by Chris Jennings Dixon © 2007 National Council of Teachers of English.

Figure 7.3

LESSON 69
AN ADVERTISING CAMPAIGN: USING RHETORICAL APPEALS

Miles McCrimmon

Purpose

- To analyze advertising methods
- To practice rhetorical approaches in persuasive writing

Preparation

When writing teachers use ads for instruction, they usually ask merely for passive analysis of advertisers' methods, allowing students to remain squarely in the consumer mode. Encouraging students to create as well as consume advertising can lead to more creative thinking and writing. Some basic work with the Aristotelian rhetorical appeals using sample advertisements (print, television, or Web) gets things started. The students need time to find examples of their own.

Props/Materials

- Videotaped sample ads and magazines
- Advertising Assignment handout (Figure 7.4)

Process/Procedure

1. Teacher distributes the Advertising Assignment handout to students to review three-step process for creating an advertising campaign.
2. The class discusses four rhetorical appeals: logos, pathos, ethos, mythos.
3. Students survey choices consumers have in a particular market segment.
4. Students review existing advertising campaigns of three brands in a product field with particular attention to the use of rhetorical approaches.
5. Students design an advertising campaign for a product using a variety of rhetorical appeals.

Pointers or Pitfalls

Usually, the assignment can be completed over a four-week period. Halfway toward the due date for the draft, it's a good idea to require an advertising analysis of at least three of the ads that will appear in Part 2 of the paper to make sure students are on the right track. Leave time at the end of the assignment for the students to present their campaigns orally and visually. Consider requiring these presentations as group assignments if you want a ready-made collaborative exercise. This activity can be as small or as large as you want to make it.

Ponderings

When my students truly inhabit the mind of the advertising copywriter, they come away from the experience far less susceptible and far more critically disposed to understand the power of consumerism.

Advertising Assignment

"Corporation A" (to be named or identified by you) has hired you as an advertising/marketing consultant. You are charged with reviewing existing brands and advertising techniques in the product field and creating a new marketing campaign. Here are some examples of product fields (but please feel free to come up with your own ideas):

- Entertainment: CDs, movies, TV shows, or video games
- Automotive: Cars, trucks, motorcycles
- Electronics: Computers, gadgets, etc.
- Communication: Cell phone contracts, beepers, pagers, etc.
- Tobacco or alcohol
- Food and Beverage: Prepared Foods, Fast Food Chains, Groceries
- Weight-Loss and Exercise Programs
- Beauty Products: Hair, Skin, Perfume, etc.
- Political Candidates
- Credit Cards and Financial Services
- Pharmaceuticals: Allergies, Depression, ADHD, Erectile Dysfunction, etc.

Part 1: Report on Brands in Product Field
For the purposes of this assignment, you may choose to market an existing company's product, or you may decide to make up an entirely new company. Regardless of what you decide, after determining the product you will be marketing, perform a brief survey of the current array of choices consumers have. Find out the market share of the product field's various brands and outline the basic, objective differences between the brands' product features, cost per unit and measurable quality.

Part 2: Review of Existing Advertising Campaigns in Product Field
Perform a detailed analysis of at least three brands' advertising methods and campaigns, including those from the corporation that has hired you as a consultant (if you are marketing an existing company's product). Remember to cite and use as many different types of advertising as you can: Web sites, radio/TV spots, magazine ads, billboards, direct mailings, etc.

In your analysis, comment on how both verbal and visual techniques in the ads use the following rhetorical appeals:

- Logos: facts, statistics, logic, reason
- Pathos: emotions (usually hope or fear or some derivation thereof)

Figure 7.4

Figure 7.4 continued

- Ethos: the company's own credibility, reputation, tradition, trustworthiness
- Mythos: commonly shared cultural beliefs like patriotism and religion

Speculate as accurately as you can on the exact demographic profile of the audience being attracted (age, gender, race, education, income, marital status, homeowner/renter, urban/suburban/rural, geographic region, etc.), and discuss the tone (the relative level of formality or informality) each company takes toward the audience and the attitude it takes toward the product or its competitors (positive, negative, neutral). You may even want to do some field research by surveying friends and relatives who are in the target demographic for the product and ask them about their image of each brand.

Part 3: Design of New Advertising Campaign
In this culmination of your study of the product field, your company's competitors, and the market, design a comprehensive advertising campaign for your company's product. Suggest media and venues for advertising, and create—with as much verbal and visual detail as possible—examples of the types of advertising you are recommending. After presenting the campaign, give the company an idea of how the strategies you are employing (the demographic share of the market being addressed, the rhetorical appeals being employed, etc.) will translate into better sales for the product. Be sure to account for frugality and feasibility in your campaign. (Don't spend $50 million if you can help it!)

Lesson Plans for Teaching Writing edited by Chris Jennings Dixon © 2007 National Council of Teachers of English.

LESSON 70
"ALL APOLOGIES": ANALYZING SONG LYRICS

Melissa Revel

Purpose

- To analyze song lyrics using a reader response approach
- To practice writing song lyrics

Preparation

Access the song lyrics freely available online at www.tekst.us/Nirvana/In-Utero/All-Apologies/ to provide copies for students. Using a search for Kurt Cobain, Nirvana front man and grunge rock star, you can find information about his life and explanations of his lyrics. His *Journals*, a collection of unedited thoughts, letters, rough drafts, diary entries, and cartoons revealing the inner workings of a troubled mind, are available at www.overstock.com.

Props/Materials

"All Apologies" from Nirvana (lyrics by Kurt Cobain)

Process/Procedure

1. The teacher accesses the song lyrics from the Internet and provides copies for the students.
2. In advance of the activity, students are requested not to blurt out the name of the band that sings the song, if they know it.
3. The teacher solicits a volunteer to read the lyrics aloud.
4. Students are asked to write what the lyrics mean to them.
5. The teacher can provide background information on the author, Kurt Cobain.
6. Students who may already be familiar with the lyrics and music of Cobain should be encouraged to contribute their understanding of his work.
7. The teacher plays a recording of "All Apologies."
8. The teacher assigns students to write their own lyrics to the tune of "All Apologies."

Pointers or Pitfalls

You must be willing to openly discuss Kurt Cobain's creative yet despairing life that ended in suicide on April 4, 1994. It can get a little sticky, but read up about him and his contributions to music before you begin this lesson (www.deathofkurtcobain.com/). Students always have many questions about how Cobain lived and died and what led him to his death.

Ponderings

I love this lesson because you can connect with the students and let them know that there is always a safe place for them to discuss what is happening in their lives. The students need to know that there are adults who are willing to listen to them and their problems. It helps them see that even famous people who seem to have it all have problems too.

LESSON 71
ARTHURIAN NEWSPAPER: JOURNALISM BASICS

Michelle Huff

Purpose

- To identify roles of newspaper staff and basic parts of the newspaper
- To develop skills in writing in newspaper format
- To demonstrate understanding of Arthurian legends

Preparation

To reinforce student understanding of the Arthurian legends, students read material in their text on Arthurian legend along with "Sir Gawain and the Green Knight." They may view videos on the legends and access background material from the Internet. Additionally, students review local newspapers to identify roles of newspaper staff and basic parts of the newspaper.

Props/Materials

Chart paper, newspapers, markers, Internet access

Process/Procedure

1. Students are divided into groups of four or five.
2. Students self-assign the roles of newspaper staff members to group members:

   Layout Person—prepares design of the newspaper

   Managing Editor—assigns stories and oversees progress

   Section Editors—brainstorm story ideas, review stories for special sections, such as Sports and Leisure

   Art Director—assigns graphics and oversees progress

3. The teacher assigns all students to be reporters and provides due dates for tasks.
4. Newspaper requirements for each group may include three obituaries, two advertisements, four news articles, two features, and one editorial.
5. Using modern newspaper format and accessing the Internet as needed, students collaboratively produce a newspaper relevant to the Arthurian time period.
6. At the end of the activity, a peer evaluation is conducted of each group's product.

Pointers or Pitfalls

Use incremental due dates or many students will let all the work pile up until the end and then panic. First, assign an outline due date and then add story due dates, layout due date, and final project due date. An alternative set of assignments needs to be prepared for those who miss time with their group when others have to fill in for them.

Ponderings

This is a highly motivational activity because those who are reticent to participate in class come to life during this time and seem to feel very proud of their efforts and final newspaper product.

LESSON 72
BEOWULF MOVIE POSTER: VISUALIZING CHARACTERIZATION

Michelle Huff

Purpose

- To develop skill in visualizing character
- To conceptualize scenes from an epic

Preparation

Students have read and discussed in class the epic *Beowulf*.

Props/Materials

Posters, markers, pencils, crayons, glue sticks and, if available, old magazines that may be cut up for collage work.

Process/Procedure

1. The teacher divides the class into groups of three or four students.
2. In their groups, students collaboratively design a movie poster to advertise an upcoming interpretation of *Beowulf*.
3. Students need to pick appropriate modern actors to fill the roles of the characters.

   Examples: Laurence Fishburne as Beowulf or David Spade as Unferth.

4. Each group works collaboratively on the movie poster to re-create images from a selected scene in *Beowulf*.
5. Students use graphics and wording to advertise the film.
6. The poster project is presented for class viewing and display.

Pointers or Pitfalls

Some students complain that they have no artistic talent, but some of the most appealing products often exhibit very primitive techniques. Working in the collage format can help those students feel more comfortable expressing themselves artistically.

Ponderings

I am always amazed at the variety and cleverness with which most of my students embrace this activity. It is a great way to get many nonverbal students to open up. This activity can be adapted to any literary work.

LESSON 73
VIDEO FREEZE CLIPS: WRITING FROM FILM

Dale DeSarro

Purpose

- To use multimedia, in this case film, as a springboard for student writing.

Preparation

Students should have already practiced some creative writing and at least one analysis of literature essay and should be familiar with analytical style as well as the creative process.

Props/Materials

TV, VCR, or DVD player; video or DVD cued to desired scene(s); paper and pen.

Process/Procedure

1. Students watch five- to seven-minute video clip (with no instructions other than to pay close attention).
2. Students write from memory all the details they can recall.
3. Students then watch the clip again adding any details they missed.
4. From these details, each student writes a narrative of the scene and shares it with the class (call on just a few volunteers to read their narratives to show the differences in interpretations).

5. Students continue along their own storylines from there and finish their stories.

Pointers or Pitfalls

If the teacher polls the class ahead of time, it is easier to find a movie that few or none of the students have seen.

Ponderings

Students enjoy being creative but find it difficult to begin. Because they are so visually stimulated, they often forget that movies begin as writing. This is one way to show that everything begins with words. I also use this type of springboard in a *Finding Forrester* style . . . presenting the beginning paragraph of a random book and having the students write from there.

LESSON 74
FILM REVIEWS: SUPPORTING OPINIONS

Stuart D. Noel

Purpose

- To practice opinionated writing that incorporates reasons and examples

Preparation

Discussion, practice, and feedback in writing film reviews. Ask students to bring in film reviews for discussion of content and organization. Use a brief film in class as a model for what to look for and what to convey in writing a film review.

Props/Materials

- Films seen in class and outside of class
- Professional film reviews
- American Film Institute Top 100 website (www.afi.com/tvevents/100years/movies.aspx)

Process/Procedure

1. The teacher provides samples of professional film reviews for students to read and identify style, structure, and content.

2. With teacher approval, each student selects a film currently showing in the theater, on video or DVD, on cable/television, or on American Film Institute's Top 100 films. (Access American Film Website for 100 Greatest Movies of All Time)

3. The teacher guides students in completing Film Review Assignment:

   - Choose the required number of films to see outside of class (either currently showing in theaters, film festivals, special showings, or from American Film Institute's Top 100) and write at least a one-page evaluation of each film.

   - What inspired you to see the film?

   - Was it what you expected? Why or why not?

   - Write as if you are a film critic. Provide specific examples to support your ideas from the film.

   - Would you see the film again? Would you recommend it to a friend?

4. Students write their reviews using specific illustrations from the films.

5. Students may incorporate opinions, but they are required to support their opinions with criteria, reasons, examples, etc.

6. Students share their reviews with peers to promote or deter others from seeing the films.

7. Each student repeats the process with a second film of his or her choice from the Top 100 list.

8. Teacher instructs students to turn in their reviews throughout the semester or at the end of semester.

Pointers or Pitfalls

The reviews tend to improve greatly as the students gain experience in analyzing film and conveying their impressions.

Ponderings

The American Film Institute's Top 100 American films is a good starting point for discussion of what makes a film a classic.

LESSON 75
DIVERSITY IN AMERICA: WRITING A MOVIE CRITIQUE

Ann Louise Johnston

Purpose

- To develop skill in reading and writing movie reviews

Preparation

Discuss a current movie with the students. Ask students to brainstorm criteria that should be used to evaluate when they praise or criticize in the movie. Elicit their reactions to recent choices for the best movie and best actor and actress at the most recent Oscar awards. Do they agree with the award selections? Why or why not? Direct students to use the Internet Movie Database website at www.imdb.com to complete this activity successfully.

Props/Materials

- Diversity Movie List at www.imdb.com/keyword/diversity/
- Teacher and student access to a computer with Internet access
- Preparation for Movie Critique: Internet Movie Database and Worksheet handout (Figure 7.5)
- Movie Critique handout (Figure 7.6)

Process/Procedure

1. Each student chooses a movie from the Diversity Movie List handout that he or she has NOT seen.

2. Before students view their movies, the teacher directs them to access the Internet Movie Database website to complete the accompanying handout.

3. The teacher reviews the Internet Movie Database and Worksheet handout with students to ensure they understand how to navigate the site to obtain data.

4. Students write their responses to the prompts.

5. The teacher reviews the Movie Critique handout with students.

6. After students have gathered information about their movies, read critiques, watched their movies, and answered evaluation sheets, they write their first drafts.

7. Students write their drafts in class using notes from worksheets.

8. Students share their writing with their peers in reader/writer groups.

9. Students edit and revise their drafts based upon peer responses to their writing and self-assessment strategies.

10. Students hand in their final movie critiques with all worksheets and drafts.

11. The teacher presents opportunities for students to share their findings in oral and/or published versions, e.g., bulletin board displays.

Pointers or Pitfalls

Be sure that students have not seen the movie before and that they all look at different movies. If they cannot find the one they have chosen, allow them to choose another. Students tend to focus too much on plot and not enough on evaluation. Be sure to limit their plot summaries to five sentences.

Ponderings

This activity also works well with biographic movies.

Preparation for Movie Critique: Internet Movie Database and Worksheet

Hand in your responses to theses items with your paragraph.

What movie did you choose in class? _____

Before You See the Movie
1. Go to the Internet and open www.imdb.com At the left hand side of the page under *Search the data base,* Click *All,* scroll down to title, click it, then in the space below enter your movie title.
2. At the left-hand side of the page, choose *plot summary* and read it. What do you expect will happen in the movie?
3. Choose *plot key words.* List ten of these words.
4. Look at the *newsgroup reviews.* Read one.
   Who is the author?_____
   Does the author suggest that you see the movie? _____
5. Look at the *external reviews.* Read one. Who is the author or what is the magazine or newspaper?_____Date?_____ Does the author suggest that you see the movie?_____What rating does he/she give?_____
6. Open up the *cast and crew.* Choose two of the actors or actresses and write their names here_____ _____.
7. Go back to the main menu. Choose *bio* by clicking on it. Then write the name of an actor or actress from Question 6. Click on *go.* From the list, look for a mini biography and read it. What have you learned about the actor or actress?
8. What is the family rating of the movie?
9. What category is the movie?
10. Go back to the main menu of the data base. Go to *Search database* and click *All,* choose *plot* and click. Write in the name of a type of plot (mystery, western, romance, adventure, science fiction, biography, horror, etc.). Click *go.* From the list of movies, write the titles of four that you have not seen that look interesting.

After You Have Seen the Movie
1. Would most students be able to understand the plot/story of the movie? Why?
2. Was the rating assigned to the movie appropriate? Why?
3. What part of the movie did you enjoy the least? Why?
4. What part of the movie did you enjoy the most? Why?
5. Name one impression that the movie showed you about American culture.
6. Evaluate the plot. How did it move from scene to scene?
   Was it believable? Did it move slowly, quickly, or just right? Did it grab the watcher's attention or was it boring?
7. Consider the main actors and actresses. Did they do a good job? Why or why not?
8. What was the setting? Did the setting fit the movie?
9. Would you recommend the movie to other students? Why or why not?

Lesson Plans for Teaching Writing edited by Chris Jennings Dixon © 2007 National Council of Teachers of English.

Figure 7.5

Movie Critique

Purpose: Watch a movie from the "Diversity Movie List" and write a critique explaining why the movie should be recommended to your classmates or why it should not be recommended to them.

Paragraph Organization

Introductory sentence: This should have the name of the movie and attract the reader's interest.

Body: This should have specific information and details evaluating the movie.

Concluding sentence: This should conclude with a generalization of why students should or should not see the movie.

Include the following information in your paragraph:

Movie Title:

Summary of the plot/ story/main idea (this should be no more than five sentences):

Main actors/actresses (name at least two):

Setting (time period, city, state, geographical area of the United States):

Film category (choose one—action adventure, children/family, comedy, drama, horror, musical, mystery/suspense, science fiction/fantasy, westerns):

Ratings
G: general audience
PG: parental guidance
PG-13: parental guidance, for children over thirteen
R: restricted to adults

Answer the following questions in your evaluation paragraph:
1. Would most students be able to understand the plot/story of the movie?
2. Was the rating assigned to the movie appropriate?
3. What part of the movie did you enjoy the least?
4. What part of the movie did you enjoy the most?
5. Name one impression that the movie showed you about American culture.

Lesson Plans for Teaching Writing edited by Chris Jennings Dixon © 2007 National Council of Teachers of English.

Figure 7.6

Appendix A: Why Institutions Need to Cross-Pollinate

Chris Jennings Dixon
Project Director, FIPSE Writing Coalition; Professor Emeritus, Tidewater Community College, Virginia Beach Campus, Virginia

> *"If I hadn't done FIPSE, I would be teaching to the test."*
> Project Participant

As you flip through this text searching for tomorrow's teaching idea, may you discover "just the right" approach to focus upon writing in your classroom. These strategies have been developed by teachers from middle schools, high schools, colleges, and universities in a collaborative Writing Coalition Project funded by the Fund for the Improvement of Postsecondary Education (FIPSE) to improve student readiness for success in college composition.

Teachers have been the crux of this project that began with a simple question: "Why are high school students unprepared for college courses?" Teachers have come together to investigate the problem and explore remedies. Teachers have empowered their students and themselves through reflective practices. And teachers have found not only answers but also developed innovative strategies. Although teachers often feel they have "stolen" ideas when they take an activity they have read about or heard discussed by others and then adapt it for their students, they are the true crafters of pedagogy, discovering what works in the classroom and finding the "teachable moment." Through their participation in collaborative activities, teachers have shared their backgrounds, their concerns, their successes, and even their failures, all in order to illuminate what happens when professionals collaborate across institutional lines for student success.

Overcoming Barriers

This text is the result of over seven years of collaboration among secondary and postsecondary English faculties that began in the spring of

1998 at Tidewater Community College (TCC), Virginia Beach Campus, Virginia, when Alma Hall, a Salem High School (SHS) English department chairperson, knocked on the door to open discussion. It all began with her inquiry about the college's method of placing students in dual enrollment classes and college remedial composition courses. That inquiry became the jumping-off point for exploration of collaborative initiatives with support from TCC and Virginia Beach City Public Schools (VBCPS) and funding from FIPSE for two comprehensive projects (1998–2001; 2001–2005) to explore solutions and disseminate results: the first project was co-directed by Chris Jennings Dixon and Ann Woolford-Singh, and the second was directed solely by Chris.

Fear of the "blame game" was an initial barrier to collaboration. Unfamiliar with placement procedures used by the college, high school teachers worried they would be found at fault for the shortcomings of freshmen college students. Questioning the high school curriculum and standards for graduation, college instructors were concerned that high school teachers would not accept them as partners. As high school students enrolled in college and found their writing skills deemed deficient by college placement tests, high school teachers asked, "What is it you want my students to be able to do?" High school and college teachers felt disconnected from the other's institution and wondered if they would have administrative support to try new approaches to writing instruction. Although surveys and research confirmed the need to open dialogue, teachers were initially suspicious of yet another mandate from afar, especially in light of ever-increasing accountability requirements brought on by high-stakes testing. They raised the question, "How can you be innovative in a structured environment?"

Beginning Dialogue

To create an atmosphere of sharing and trust, a team approach evolved. Composed of four to five high school English teachers (including the high school English Department chair) and a college composition instructor, each team scheduled weekly one-hour meetings outside of school hours to exchange professional and personal concerns and plan ways to help students develop skills and confidence in writing. One problem among the teachers soon emerged, "We're so busy." Yes, the secondary teachers and college instructors were committed individuals already involved in numerous professional activities. Fortunately, grant funding enabled dedicated project personnel to receive monetary compensation for their efforts to resurrect additional reserves of energy and time to develop innovative approaches to writing instruction. As college instructor and project participant, Charles W. Hoofnagle found, "When student learning is the motivator, educators—even those of diverse backgrounds—will pull together to find a way to promote, encourage, and ultimately achieve real learning."

One of the first high school partners, Ted Telle, who now teaches for the Department of Overseas Education in Germany, relates his team-member memories at SHS,

> When I began the FIPSE project, I was a typical, by-the-book type of teacher. When I was accepted into the project in the summer of 1998, I was excited to be involved in a project to help students actually improve their writing skills. I liked sharing the daily workings in Room 206 and helping all the kids. Not so much the "big picture stuff" but the "teachable moments," when the light came on for the kids.

While high school teachers gained a better perspective on what their students would face in college writing assignments, college faculty acquired renewed respect for the challenges of teaching in a high school setting. Joanne Diddlemeyer, TCC/Norfolk Dean of Languages, Mathematics, and Sciences, describes her experience as a project team leader,

> At one of our meetings, we discussed portfolios and where to go with them, in other words how to develop a vertical portfolio for the whole school. The discussion was so much fun that we ended up staying for over two hours! Thank you for getting me involved in this project. Each week after the roundtables, I get so excited about what we're doing in education and it just gives me the momentum to push forward!

Expanding Partnerships

Sharing features of the project model and results of collaboration at state and national conferences ignited interest and inquiries from remote institutions. As the first three-year project came to a conclusion, high school teachers Jane Hunn, Ted Telle, Diana Olmstead, and Nancy Kubu, in partnership with TCC college leader Chris Jennings Dixon, collected, formatted, and arranged for college printing of two volumes of strategies for teaching writing and establishing writing centers. These in-house publications were shared locally and nationally in workshop and conference presentations. Dissemination of the publications along with information on the project and attendant results stimulated applications from instructional leaders in VBCPS, the Virginia Community College System, and national postsecondary sites to become future partners.

Supported by TCC, FIPSE project director Jennings Dixon wrote and submitted a second FIPSE grant application for dissemination of the model. In fall 2001, the U.S. Department of Education awarded TCC a second FIPSE grant to foster institutionalization and dissemination of the proven successful model in ten geographically dissimilar sites. The goals were (1) promote partnerships to improve communication between secondary and postsecondary institutions to increase student learning opportunities; (2) provide opportunities for high school and college English faculties to collaborate in professional workshops to develop and implement innovative instructional strategies; (3) develop alignment between secondary and postsecondary institutions through a deliberate articulation of composition-related curriculum and instruction; (4) reduce the number of high school graduates needing remediation in writing prior to enrolling in college composition classes; and (5) implement successful reform initiatives through a transfer of knowledge and strategies to a variety of adapting sites to improve quality and accessibility to postsecondary education for diverse student populations.

Using a multitiered approach, the TCC Writing Coalition continued its existing relationship with VBCPS to showcase partners and expanded locally to include teachers and students from additional high schools and colleges in the region. National project sites were selected based upon already established networks for collaboration: instructional programs, such as dual enrollment; shared literary publications; histories of academic partnerships. Prospective college and university site leaders were interviewed to determine their levels of interest in working with high schools, and letters of support for collaboration were tendered by secondary and postsecondary administrations.

Through the FIPSE Writing Coalition, ten two-year and four-year institutions in eight states joined in partnership with secondary schools in their surrounding areas to align writing instruction: Tidewater Community College, Virginia, with Green Run, Kellam, Landstown, and Salem High Schools; J. Sargeant Reynolds Community College (JSRCC), Virginia, with Lee Davis High School; John Tyler Community College (JTCC), Virginia, with Lloyd C. Bird High School; Arizona State University (ASU) with Sam Fees Middle School; California State University (CSU), Fullerton, with Buena Park High School; Florida Community College, Jacksonville (FCCJ) with Wolfson High School; Forsyth Technical Community College (FTCC), North Carolina with Parkland High School; Georgia Perimeter College (GPC) with Towers High School; Greenville Tech College (GTC), South Carolina with Woodmont High School; and Southwestern Michigan College (SWM) with Ross

Beatty High School. Student populations varied from CSU's Orange County, where many students speak Spanish or a dialect of Chicano English, to GPC's metropolitan Atlanta setting characterized by the Afro-American economically disadvantaged, to SWM's rural, sparsely populated agricultural region, to ASU's partnership with American Indian descendents in a middle school then classified as "under performing" by the Arizona State public school standards.

Creating a Culture of Innovation

The partners were organized in a "hub and spokes" relationship with the TCC Writing Coalition directed by Jennings Dixon at the center. Working directly with the project director and receiving resources to adapt and refine regional approaches to collaboration, each partner developed its own variation of the TCC model. Postsecondary and secondary teachers used the roundtable model to meet an hour before or after school or in two-hour blocks or in half-day sessions. Marty Brooks, FTCC leader, relates, "At every session, teachers reported on what activities they had used during their classes from the 'Activity Checklist,' a list that they had agreed to follow. They discussed which exercises did and did not work. They also discussed how they implemented ideas from the professional development workshops in their classes." At Woodmont High School, former English department chair and now instructional assistant Chris Smutzer relates, "Once we as high school teachers realized that a large percentage of our seniors were not as prepared for college as we thought, the issue of grade inflation was discussed. Essentially, we concluded that teachers had not held students accountable enough for writing deficiencies and had awarded too much credit for 'effort' and lower-level thinking, such as memorization, as apposed to analysis, evaluation, and synthesis." Site leader Susan Slavicz, FCC/J, comments, "What really surprised me as a college instructor was how eager the high school teachers were for information. Far from feeling like an interloper, I felt that my input was welcomed and helpful. I was also surprised that the instructors were interested in testing their seniors. With all of the testing being used in schools right now, I assumed that would be the last thing anyone would want." At Buena Park High School, Jennifer Fletcher, project teacher adds, "We share a common educational philosophy and common teaching practices, and we work toward a common goal—the empowerment of all students to be informed and critical participants in our society."

Sharing ideas in teaching teams and opening up classrooms for demonstration created a culture for experimentation with teacher roles that promote student accountability. At the GPC/Towers site, Kelly Duncan, a social studies team member, reflects, "I was concerned about being a social studies teacher and not an English teacher, but I believe that all teachers, regardless of area, can and should be teachers of writing." As a result of participation, Duncan relates, "I have taken more risks as a teacher because I now have a better understanding of assessing and grading student writing." Implementing new approaches, Bird High School team member Susan Bolton comments, "The student memo has given students an opportunity to communicate with me in a non-threatening way. I have found that the student memo makes me aware of problems, challenges, and successes students have had. This means that communication is now a very important part of my classroom." Jennifer Mohorter, Lee Davis High School teacher, adds, "My classroom has been a laboratory this year, and my students the guinea pigs . . . one innovation that was successful this year was the digital writing portfolio. During the process, my role as teacher changed from facilitator/instructor to 'peer.'"

Along with regular communication and site visits by the project director, the Writing Coalition hosted annual workshops in Virginia Beach to bring remote college and university project site leaders and secondary teachers together to share progress and brainstorm strategies. One participant capsulizes the experience, "As teachers, we share within our school and department, but being able to share with teachers from other schools only deepens the pool of our resources."

Shifting the Focus

Using activities from the project model, each secondary school developed strategies for its respective curricular needs to align writing instruction with its partnering postsecondary institution. At SHS, the FIPSE partnership was extended from the English department to a writing-across-the-curriculum approach for students in government classes taught by Dave Meyerholz. Meyerholz began tentatively with some ideas about including student writing in his lesson plans; however, by the end of the grant period, he was committed to the writing process. He notes:

> One of the unfortunate trends in teaching seniors, in my view, is that we educators have officially and formally acknowledged that longtime springtime affliction of "senioritis," which starts in Janu-

ary of one's junior year. I became convinced that some formal writing assignment should end the school year (and, for seniors, their high school careers) that brings their educational experiences into perspective. I, therefore, designed a writing assignment "The Final Word Is Yours" that concludes the academic careers of most of my students.

Likewise, faculty at all dissemination sites responded positively to collaboration and discovered innovative approaches to improving student readiness for college-level composition. SWC project site leader Joe Lemrow reports that the focus of much of his department's daily discussion changed after his college chose to participate in the FIPSE project, "Colleagues now routinely discuss student writing behaviors and ways to address student-writing problems." Bird teacher Bolton comments, "I have gained the most from learning expectations of college instructors so that I can better prepare students. The strategies others have shared have also made a difference in what I do in class." JSRCC site leader Miles McCrimmon adds, "When the FIPSE grant gave us the opportunity for routine interaction, the veils of ignorance fell pretty quickly. When we gave each other tacit permission to fail, we began to try new things and learned that we could innovate while still maintaining high standards."

Teacher-Designed Workshops

To promote meaningful conversations, the teams planned and facilitated professional development workshop activities each semester in response to topics initiated in roundtable discussions. Six instructional needs were identified: (1) engage students' interest in writing, (2) clearly articulate college writing requirements, (3) emphasize instruction on editing and proofreading, (4) clarify requirements of the state assessment tool, i.e. Virginia Standards of Learning, (5) revise syllabi to include collaborative writing strategies, and (6) develop ongoing teacher self-assessment. Sessions were usually scheduled at noninstructional sites where participants discarded institutional titles, convened informally in roundtable settings, brainstormed and reflected upon teaching practices, and continued lively repartees over box lunches. Collaboratively, they identified what they valued in writing and what they expected of their students. Fran Sharer, VBCPS instructional specialist, comments, "After spending some time in discussion getting to know the TCC faculty, it became very clear that we all had the same goal—student success through improved writing." TCC participant Bonnie Startt recalls, "It was an enlightening day as we discovered that many of our truths about 'them' were not true, and we found out why some things were done as they were."

Not only did the collaborative workshops help participants better understand the unique characteristics of the other's institution, but they also propelled teachers to experiment in their classrooms. From workshops such as "Teaching and Learning through Letters," "Classroom Management and the Revision Process," and "The Changing Role of the Instructor in the Portfolio Process," teachers developed confidence in "trying out" new approaches to writing instruction. National workshop presenters over the seven years of FIPSE funding included Kathleen Yancey, then affiliated with Clemson University, author of *Portfolios in the Writing Classroom* and *Situating Portfolios* and coeditor of *Assessing Writing*; Beverly Chin, University of Montana, author of *Grammar for Writing*; Jennifer Berger and Stephanie Dunson, The Bard Institute for Writing and Thinking; Susan Cross, University of California, Irvine, director of *Grammar from the Ground Up*; Donna Reiss, former professor TCC, coauthor of *Electronic Communication Across the Curriculum*; Joe Antinerella, TCC, coauthor of *A Class Act: Approaches and Activities for Today's English Classroom*; Sally Harrell, TCC administrator and office specialist, Office of Workforce Development; Wendy Weiner, former dean at John Tyler Community College and VCCS interim director of educational planning; and Leila Christenbury, Virginia Commonwealth University, coauthor of *Writing On Demand*.

Experimenting with Writing Assessment

Emerging as a proverbial "guiding force" for an examination of writing practices and assessment, Kathleen Yancey became the project's informal writing advisor and head cheerleader. Her work on portfolios lent further justification to another project goal—to demonstrate the effectiveness of portfolio instruction, evaluation, and placement. From October 1998, when Yancey led a FIPSE/TCC-sponsored session entitled "Engaging Student Interest in Writing and Development of Writing Portfolios," to now, portfolios have permeated secondary and postsecondary composition classrooms wherever she has presented. Jane Hunn, former SHS team member and English department chair, now a teacher in Ft. Lauderdale, Florida, recalls, "The writing consultant (Yancey) returned throughout the three years of the first FIPSE grant to work with the project teachers. In addition, she was contracted by our school system to work on a portfolio initiative with teachers in grades K–12."

Beginning in 1999 as a writing consultant for VBCPS, Yancey led sessions to train 600 teachers in portfolio methodology over a six-year period. Subsequently, a cadre of participants evolved for peer training in all schools, and every VBCPS English curriculum guide now starts with a unit on the use of portfolios.

Yancey turned the normal negative tone of "grading" or "marking" student compositions into a positive one focusing upon what a student could do well to promote more of that skill set. Reading portfolios as a whole text, teachers looked for evidence of reflection and control of language instead of comma splices and split infinitives. Teaching strategies were developed and refined following each of the all day project-sponsored workshops, usually two held per semester. Initially suspicious of the portfolio method, after exposure to the process through workshops and roundtable discussions, secondary and postsecondary teachers set aside their reservations and experimented with collection, reflection, and presentation concepts in their classrooms, as evidenced by VBCPS English teacher Randy Giordano's comment, "Previously, I do believe I'd looked upon portfolios as not much more than a filing nuisance. I have learned through the FIPSE project that the revision process teaches far more than I had given credit." Another VBCPS teacher, Glenda Anderson, shares her experience: "I used to grade like an old person. The one thing about portfolios I like is that it puts pressure on the students to complete something. One other thing the portfolios impressed on me is that the kids truly do take pride in their work when they get to rework pieces."

Through faculty participation in workshops and portfolio grading sessions, high school and college instructors became comfortable with this teaching culture. Both adjunct and full-time college instructors implemented and honed portfolio strategies in their classrooms as they discovered that their students were taking greater ownership of the writing process. TCC adjunct instructor Tom Hargrove relates that he views "the portfolio approach as a highly flexible and powerful teaching tool; to the point where it has become one of the central components in structuring most of my courses," while Sylvia Ross, TCC instructor, notes, "I have learned how to induce students to be more aware of and actually practice the writing process, particularly revision, that my high school colleagues work hard to help their students improve their writing skills, and that anything that gets students excited about writing is a good thing and worthy of academic discussion. Compared to the traditional writing classroom, students in the portfolio classroom live in an extended writing process."

Using Assessment to Identify Good Writing

Not only did portfolios provide an important link between institutions, the approach promoted innovations in assessment. The routine testing practice at TCC, and many colleges across the nation, requires all entering students be placed in writing, reading, and mathematics courses by COMPASS, a multiple-choice, commercially developed, computerized assessment tool. The writing section is essentially an editing test of a few selected pieces. If a student's score falls into a borderline "gray" placement area, he or she may be required to write to a prompt for twenty minutes. As an aside, with the need to ensure student readiness for timed writing samples, "Writing on Demand" strategies were identified and refined for classroom use to provide opportunities for students to practice writing to a prompt in a limited time period; however, the use of a single indicator and/or a timed writing sample for demonstration of a student's readiness for college work was and remains a concern of students and teachers who utilize the writing process in their classrooms.

Through workshop experiences, facilitators led secondary and postsecondary teachers to an appreciation of portfolios, to a commitment to introduce and refine portfolio methodologies in their classrooms, and to an exploration of authentic multiple measures of assessment. Following TCC's initial experimentation with the use of SHS seniors' portfolios as an alternative placement method, the program was made available to four project schools and subsequently to all thirteen VBCPS high schools. To support this methodology, over thirty high school and college teachers were trained each year in development and use of rubrics, anchors, and scoring guides to evaluate senior-year portfolios and use the assessments for college placement in developmental and college-transfer writing courses. Dale DeSarro, Green Run High School English 12 teacher and department co-chair praises the motivational factor: "Prior to my involvement with the FIPSE program, I was constantly bombarded with 'Why are we doing this?' and 'How is this going to affect me in the real world?' With the portfolio placement aspect of the project, I had a carrot to dangle, an actual concrete reward besides the grade they would earn. As the project came to a close, that 'reward' was no longer necessary, but it was a way to get them started."

Portfolio readings demonstrated an increased understanding among educators of what student skills are necessary for college work. At the TCC site, high school and college instructors who participated in readings of over three hundred portfolios each year repeatedly demonstrated over 92 percent inter-reader reliability rates. Sylvia Brooks,

English teacher at Bird who also participated in the TCC portfolio readings, comments, "Participating in the grading of portfolios in April at Tidewater was fascinating. I also enjoyed hearing the other teachers talk about their students and programs. I truly believe that a portfolio assessment is the best indicator of a student's writing."

Likewise, Kacey Ruckstaetter, TCC instructor, shares her firsthand experience as a portfolio reader:

> I had never been in a session like this, where there were so many opinions about how to evaluate the portfolios. What if the portfolio wasn't complete? How do you evaluate poetry as an entry in the portfolio? What if the narrative was so personal that it read more like a journal entry than a paper? What if two portfolios from different students were alike? These questions all spurred many opinions from the instructors, and a heated discussion continued on the portfolios until a general consensus had been met. The most important thing I learned from the norming session, at least about grading portfolios, is that even though sometimes grading writing is subjective, it is possible for a group of English instructors to come to a consensus on what constitutes good writing.

During the grant period, high school project students presented oral readings of outstanding pieces from their portfolios for an audience of peers, faculty, and families at a Virginia Beach Barnes & Noble Book Store each spring. TCC project staff presented certificates for outstanding work and college writing handbooks to the honorees. Administrative support for the event was evidenced by the high school principal's attendance and funding gifts of appreciation for recognized students.

Propagating Portfolios

The FIPSE Writing Coalition also assisted in making arrangements for Yancey to present workshops exploring print and digital portfolios at multiple national project sites. Many dissemination sites found the portfolio to be a fundamental element of collaboration and a vehicle for alignment of writing. At SMC, Lemrow expresses surprise in the delay between initiating and implementing portfolio ideas at Ross Beatty, "Because many individuals could not conceive of a need for a separate writing portfolio, many hours were spent defining the need, deciding which tasks should be included, which tasks were representative of ability, which teachers would have to modify assignments to meet portfolios norms, etc." GTC site leader Susan P. Allen reports from discussions with Woodmont teachers, "The attitude toward portfolios is positive; however, no real strides have been made in their implementation," while at Bird High School, JTCC project site leader Brooks describes the teachers' renewed focus upon writing, "In particular, the faculty wished to focus on assignments that encouraged revision, self-reflection, and that allowed students to use their required writing folders as more than repositories for their writing." Bird teacher Susan S. Hawkes comments, "FIPSE workshops and the debates over the portfolio encouraged me to increase self-reflection activities in my new assignments." Another teacher participant Mohorter reflects, "I am getting better at preparing my students for life outside the Lee Davis walls, even if it didn't involve college. Whether or not the digital portfolio worked with my students was not the issue anymore; they were writing and because of it, they were better writers."

At the conclusion of the FIPSE grant, TCC supported the portfolio project for area VBCPS senior English students for one year; however, problems in administration affected continuation of the program as observed by TCC professor Charles S. Pierce, "Often administrators do not want to pay for the work involved and prefer an automated test, such as COMPASS, which may be cheaper." Administrators seem to view the portfolio activity as labor intensive, unwieldy, and yet another item to add to their already overextended budgets. Despite the validation for authentic assessment provided by the portfolio placement methodology and its attendant demonstration of success for students and teachers, institutionalization of this approach requires identification of additional sources of funding, re-energizing secondary and postsecondary staff, and renewed administrative direction.

Establishing a Writing Center

An extremely popular by-product of the FIPSE Writing Coalition Project was establishment of high school writing centers because of their visibility and potential to promote writing-across-the-curriculum reform. To provide a writing community, an extended audience for student writing, and practice in self-assessment and reflection, TCC assisted area high schools in establishing writing centers based upon the college model. The college and project staff provided resource materials, conducted role modeling activities in high school classrooms to train prospective high school student consultants, and hosted workshops for teachers on tutor training.

The SHS team cordoned off a third of a classroom, painted walls, made signs, located round tables to promote writing conversations, and arranged for computer and telephone hook-up to access the TCC online and Grammar Hotline facilities. Hunn describes the steps teachers took to establish the writing center:

> To staff the writing center, teachers were released from other non-teaching duties. Project teachers tutored voluntarily in the center before and after school and during lunch breaks. One teacher was designated as the center director. His duties included scheduling teachers to staff the center, obtaining and monitoring student consultants, coordinating student consultant training, overseeing and securing resources, scheduling bulletin board displays, tracking attendance, preparing presentations to showcase the center, and establishing a system of rewards to encourage students to frequently visit the center. We had a motto for our writing center: "It's a Life Saver." When students completed a writing session, they received LifeSavers candy as well as valuable practice in understanding the writing process.

Project team member Ramona Clark describes the Green Run center:

> The writing center is located in the library—a perfect location. We have several computers in the center, and the atmosphere is conducive and friendly. English teachers man the writing center during all lunches and study blocks in lieu of another duty, and this works well. The whole faculty has been advised of the writing center's existence and has been encouraged to take advantage of it. As a matter of fact, department chairs received a packet of information to share with their departments. In order for the writing center experience to impact the instructional experience more, there needs to be an incentive. Some teachers offer extra credit or just flat out require their students to visit the center. At the beginning of the year, we have an orientation to the writing center.

Elizabeth H. Beagle, coordinator of the Landstown center located at the end of a hallway, reflects,

> The center has become a very important extension of my classroom. I think that the best use of the center should be a way to extend what the students learn in the classroom. Overall, the student's reaction has been positive. I have encouraged my students to seek out their peers and to use the writing center as much as possible. It is encouraging to see that they are beginning to realize that the teacher is not their only resource. I believe the staff at LHS has come to realize that the center can be useful for

any subject area. We have had students from varying disciplines use the center this year. We were very pleased to launch our OWL (online writing lab) this year. Although it did not get much use, we were very happy with the initial results and have planned to continue it next year. We are going to have the center open during every lunch and study block.

Surveys of participating teachers confirm the value of their participation in this activity: "My role now is one of helper, a co-creator, an aspect that really helped through practice in the writing center," "Now when students meet with a new writing task for the first time, they do not procrastinate and shrink in fear. They simply come into our center for help. My interaction in the writing center made me glad I'm a teacher." Student consultants' surveys also affirm the value of their volunteer work: "It really feels good. Seeing the look on someone's face when they feel the relief of having completed a requirement of their paper," or "I believe it allowed me to look at my own work with a more objective eye," and "Working in the writing center helped me help others write. Because of this I improved myself."

Writing Center Spin-offs

The high school writing center emerged as a national focal point of collaboration for teachers and students. Designed as not only a one-on-one faculty/advisor experience but also as a peer-consultant enterprise, the writing center motivates student participation in the writing process. Individual schools adapted the writing center model for their sites based upon available space and staffing needs. At Parkland High School, where a center was established in a classroom in collaboration with FTCC, English Department Chair Beverly McCarthy reports, "Students and teachers in the writing center have formed a 'team' through this project." At Ross Beatty, teachers adapted a corner of their library; at Woodmont, teachers situated the center along one wall in a teacher's classroom; at Towers, teachers commandeered a portable classroom, cleaned and furnished it as a Read/Write Now Center. Brooks comments upon the Bird site, "The fact that over twenty students were peer consultants and they were eager to be scheduled suggests that there is a large segment of the student population that is interested in working with their fellow students and their writing."

Staffing writing centers can be problematic with many centers only able to offer limited hours of operation. One option that needs further study may be found at the after-school writing center at Fees Middle School supervised by graduate assistant/doctoral students from Arizona State University. ASU students provide guidance and instruction in a variety of writing projects, including assistance with writing assignments (homework), a school newspaper, and writing activities designed to enhance the writing skills as outlined in the Arizona Department of Education Standards for Writing. The middle school students do not think of their project as a writing center or remedial writing class but rather as an after-school club that they named "Fees Fire Writers' Writing Club." Guided through the portfolio process, students submit entries to literary journals and create an online literary magazine.

Utilization of space is a premium factor in writing center survival. Several high schools found their centers overtaken by administrative directives to provide services for remedial tutoring or in-school suspension. At the Bird center, teachers adjusted the mission of their writing center to assist students in passing statewide tests and received compensation through local funding. Hawkes reports, "Student use of the center has increased and students have learned to be specific about the kind of help they need. The tutors have been flexible in working with students on classroom and SOL remediation." Likewise, at Kellam, the writing center coordinator Angie Evans applied for and received a VBCPS Building Futures grant to supply materials for her center.

Some teachers expressed concern about the longevity of their writing centers. Lisa Long, former chair of the Landstown High School English Department, comments, "I do worry about being able to continue staffing a writing center as we become more and more crowded, and as demands on the classroom teacher become even greater." In response, Lee Davis teacher Mohorter recommends, "We need to really sell the lab to the other teachers in the building, then to the students. If we can have a few teachers join our campaign and jump on the soon-to-be bandwagon, we will have more success and more students seeking assistance in the lab." CSU site leader Mary Kay Crouch predicts, "I think the enthusiasm which has developed for the Buena Park writing center, which will continue after the FIPSE project is completed, indicates that the project will continue on and its influence will be felt for a long time."

Did It Work?

Each institutional partnership has developed lines of communication and contacts between postsecondary and secondary faculties to improve student preparation for college writing. Both teachers and students have benefited from the collaborative activities. Many of the college and university sites have expanded their programs to additional secondary sites and are actively developing institutional measures to support collaboration among their faculties.

McCrimmon, JSRCC site leader, predicts:

> If no master narrative emerges when I listen to teachers about what got them into the profession, what keeps them in the classroom past the two- or three-year mark is usually pretty clear: a sense of belonging to a learning community and an opportunity to collaborate in an environment that values their ideas. At our site, the single most important feature of the FIPSE grant was the invitation to collaborate in an organized fashion on a weekly basis. The teachers involved and the rewards they cite give me reason to believe they will continue to work as a collaborative long after the grant-funded stipends are a distant memory.

Identifying a large population of students from the two FIPSE projects (1998–2005), TCC's Institutional Effectiveness Office gathered and interpreted data on student placement, success, and retention. Project students were found to more frequently place into college level work using portfolios, rather than with traditional placement methods. As demonstrated in spring 2001, project students placed into freshman composition with COMPASS at a rate of 54.4 percent while a control group placed at a rate of 36.96 percent with COMPASS. More importantly, those same project students placed into freshman composition at a rate of 75.2 percent using portfolio assessments. With increased accessibility to college transfer work through the portfolio methodology, critics still questioned those students' preparation for the rigors of college work. Following the success rates (A, B, or C in coursework) of project students each year, the TCC assessment office found that project students consistently matched the performance levels of traditionally placed students. From 2001 through 2005, final placement levels into freshman composition for project students increased each year; in the last year of the FIPSE Writing Coalition, 70 percent of project students received a freshman composition placement using their senior-year portfolios. Moreover, the overall retention rate for project high school students in three identified high schools who entered TCC each fall over the period of 1999–2002 was 63 percent versus that of nonproject students' whose rate was 48 percent. Additionally, as compared to the 68 percent retention rate for all TCC students in spring 2004, the retention rate for project students in spring 2005 grew to 88 percent.

Further qualitative reflection upon the success of this project as measured by the portfolio aspect of this project is offered by Michele Marits, TCC instructor and project team member:

I emphasize "accomplishment" because these portfolios represented the unique collaboration between area high schools and TCC; they represented all we had learned from the workshops, such as those offered by Kathleen Yancey and by The Bard Institute; they represented all the collegial discussions at the roundtables and seminars; and, they represented all the years of ponderings about "what we value in a piece of writing," which culminated in the assessment rubric and the Placement Portfolio Scoring Guide. But, most-of-all, they represented students' accomplishments—students' essays, rough and final drafts, their letters to us, the readers, and their reflections on their bodies of work. We heard their "voices," their hopes and aspirations for the future, and we all became better teachers in the process.

Partnering institutions found similar results with students and teachers. Some institutions identified positive trends in student achievement via overall state-mandated writing assessments. Using pre- and post-writing samples to garner data during the secondary school year, GTC project students demonstrated a 15 percent improvement in pre- to posttests of college writing. Enlisting help from their Offices of Institutional Assessment, postsecondary institutions attempted to track the progress of their project students from high school to college; however, many sites found these data difficult to identify due to small numbers or lack of follow-up information. Fear of identify theft prompted many high school students and teachers to dismiss requests for social security numbers that are essential to acquire and manage such data. Additionally, many two-year institutions were unable to monitor performance of project students due to the transitory nature of their student bodies.

Follow-up information from the FCC-J site found thirty-eight Wolfson project graduates at the college campus in fall 2004 placing into college transfer composition courses. Of those students, 90 percent completed the course successfully, and 95 percent reenrolled for the next semester. In spring 2005, twenty-eight Wolfson project graduates enrolled in college composition for the first time, and 83 percent completed the course successfully. Totals for the year show that 90 percent of the Wolfson project students completed college composition successfully. Further encouraging data were presented by the assessment office at SMU in its review of data for Ross Beatty project graduates: "Since the FIPSE program has been in place, 100 percent of students taking English 103 (college transfer) have passed with a 'C' or above, as opposed to the 78 and 73 percent in the two years preceding the grant."

Problems and Opportunities

Politics, networking, buy-in, staying connected, and *administrative support* became buzz words in day-to-day operations of the grant project. As with any innovation, unexpected hurdles were encountered and challenges were met through adjustments and alternative strategies. Personnel changes, increasing personal responsibilities of teachers, and faculty attrition were all part of the growing pains of this project. A lack of continuity in administrative and instructional partnerships at all sites created a constantly changing canvas of educators necessitating repeated orientations, updating, and retraining. GTC site leader Allen describes the problem of maintaining momentum despite teacher turnover, "Surprising and challenging." Likewise, SMU site leader Lemrow comments on the repercussions of reassigned principals, "A good deal of time will have to be spent just to arrive at where we were." Locally, targeted high schools in VBCPS rotated staffs and altered teams. However, when one high school team "disappeared," other teams were forged. When necessary, teachers reviewed habits of group dynamics and conflict resolution. The flexibility and willingness of project staff to adapt created more opportunities for interaction among high school and college staffs. Professor Ann L. Johnston, former TCC Humanities Department chair, who had initially encouraged TCC instructors Pat Naulty, Ann Woolford-Singh, and Chris Dixon Jennings to apply for the original FIPSE grant in 1998, remained supportive throughout the ups and downs in both project periods. Johnston summarizes, "Through cooperation, teachers have learned to be better instructors. Both high school and college students have improved in their writing skills. The beginning issues were solvable. High school teachers and college teachers now better understand each other's curricula. School administrators better understand the need to produce competent writers."

To complete dissemination initiatives, the Writing Coalition project received a one-year, no cost extension from FIPSE in 2004–2005. This funding enabled participants from all ten postsecondary and secondary partnerships to review instructional strategies that had been successful in their classrooms and integrated into curriculum. In regional writing workshops, middle, high school, community college, and university teachers reflected upon common issues, identified best teaching practices, developed materials for dissemination, and recommended follow-up collaborative actions for student success.

Sharing, Borrowing, Reinventing Classroom Ideas

As Bird High School teacher Bolton remarks, "Teachers are notorious thieves! We borrow ideas from anyone who offers them." One activity that began in the TCC/SHS partnership was a letter-writing activity between high school seniors and college freshmen to gain advice on "What I Wish I Had Known Before I Came to College." At Wolfson, Marcia Heitz altered the activity to assign a letter to next year's freshmen from her senior English students. Another popular strategy was to use visual tools, such as highlighters, to match students' propensity for visual learning. Sherri Bova at Bird relates, "The kids loved highlighting the errors they found in their peer's papers, and quite a few commented that the use of color code allowed them to identify and correct errors with ease and confidence."

At the ASU/Fees site, the weekly piloting of writing activities in the center led to a collection of writing lessons. One of the most successful strategies was for the writing teacher to show students her own attempts at writing. One ASU graduate student's evaluation of this experience confirmed the value of firsthand application of classroom knowledge, "It was exciting to watch students who were uninterested and apprehensive about writing blossom into eager writers as the semester came to an end." Another commented, "If there is one thing I've learned at Fees, it is to encourage the students to write from their hearts."

Reworking strategies developed from roundtable discussions, workshop presentations, and in-class experimentation, participants from middle, high school, college and university partnerships were delighted to have one more opportunity to reconvene in collaborative settings, one of the major benefits of this project. Together they have prepared *Lesson Plans for Teaching Writing*, a compendium of instructional strategies that present real writing experiences.

Finding the Answer

Using the Writing Coalition project as an example of high school to college collaboration for her 2003 dissertation *The Journey from High School to College: Do Collaborative Connections Improve Student Transition?* Dean of Academic Instruction Billie Unger, Shepherd College, West Virginia, interviewed and researched case studies of TCC students who had been part of the high school study group. She concludes,

> The original goal of the Writing Coalition to reduce the number of students requiring college developmental English courses by

preparing them for college level English is obviously being met. Not one of the twelve students reported having felt unprepared for college English. This in itself is an endorsement of the program's success. Many of them (students) suggested that the program be replicated for other content areas, especially math. The most common suggestions provided by the participants actually pertained more to a comprehensive high school/postsecondary collaborative program than to an academic alliance. Clearly, the students longed for more interaction between high school and college students and personnel. They also alluded to their observation that if high school courses had been more challenging, their transition to college would have been much smoother.

In an evaluation of the FIPSE project, Ann Bartholomay, education coordinator and former Learning Assistance Center coordinator, Southwest Virginia Community College, summarizes,

> The values of this grant went far beyond the writing skills. Tutors developed leadership skills. Students developed social skills through a variety of different interaction experiences. Students set goals, both short range and long range. Those goals often aimed the students for college, even students who would not otherwise have made the choice.

Additionally she recommends, "The extensive professional development within this grant has brought about a spirit of togetherness among a group that spans the entire nation. The network that surely has emerged from the geographical spread has to have an effect on student learning."

"Why are students unprepared for college courses?"

Has the answer to this initial question that prompted this collaboration been found? As voiced by one high school teacher, "FIPSE has allowed me to see the challenges other teachers face when teaching writing, and I have learned that I am not the only survivor in the lifeboat." The adage "Commiseration loves company" does foster cooperative approaches, but more importantly, through collaborative activities, faculty have been brought together to effect meaningful change.

Perhaps the real solution is not a strategy or a skill-set or even an assessment tool. Working through two FIPSE projects over a seven-year period, as director, I have had the opportunity to work with teachers who have demonstrated amazing resiliency to overcome the public's finger-pointing when headlines purport "Johnny Cannot Write" or "Senior Year is Largely a Waste" and to deal with unspoken state mandates that seem to promote "Teaching to the Test." Through partnerships in Virginia, North Carolina, South Carolina, Georgia, Florida, Michigan, Arizona, and California, teachers have demonstrated a common belief in student success and diligently sought new routes for student preparation for college writing.

When teachers are given the tools and support they need to instruct, students succeed. Those who produce the tests or pen the news articles need to listen to high school and college teachers as these project participants have listened to and responded to each other. Despite time constraints and multiple social and educational issues inherent in teaching in public secondary and postsecondary schools, teachers in this project adopted a focused approach to writing instruction and altered their roles from dispensers of information to coaches of composition. While institutions seem more than willing to find funding for outside consultants, testing firms, and electronic software programs, they rarely mine the treasures within the educational institutions themselves—the teachers. Opportunities for reflection and dialogue need to be built into the fiber of educational research and measurement of student success.

Fortunately, the Writing Coalition Project enabled teachers to hear each other's voices, to reflect, and to create. Within the pages of *Lesson Plans for Teaching Writing*, we present practical instructional strategies that have worked in our classrooms.

Appendix B: Institutional Characteristics Site Information

Institution	Pop.	Demographics	Socioeconomic	Writing Assessment Tool	Aux. Funding
Arizona State University Tempe, AZ	57,000	70% White 13% Hispanic 5% Asian 4% Black 4% Unknown 3% International 2% Native American			
Buena Park High School Buena Park, CA	2,066	66% Hispanic 16% White 10% Asian/Pacific Islander 6% Black 1.5% Other	free and reduced lunch: 16.2% CalWorks: 11.5%	California English Language Development Test (CELDT) 15% grade 12 advanced 38% grade 12 early advanced 8% grade 12 early intermediate 7% grade 12 beginning Standardized Testing and Reporting (STAR): Students scoring 50% or above 46% grade 11 ELA 45% grade 11 Reading 45% grade 11 Math California High School Exit Exam (CAHSEE): Pass Rates: 69% ELA 72% MATH	Title I Title II Title IV Title V EIA-LEP* School Improvement Funds
California State University, Fullerton Fullerton, CA	32,000	39% White 22% Asian/Pacific Islander 21% Latino 9% Black 4% Native American		English Placement Test: All students after university acceptance. Exemption with SAT-550 or ACT-24 (EPT- multiple-choice items on reading and composing skills, essay requires reading passage, taking position, and supporting position with reasons and examples from experience or reading). English Writing Proficiency test: Exit exam required for graduation	

Institution	Pop.	Demographics	Socioeconomic	Writing Assessment Tool	Aux. Funding
Fees Middle School Tempe, AZ	1,071	34.17% White 34.17% Hispanic 19.23% Native American 9.62% Black 2.80% Asian	free or reduced lunch: 46.03% mobility rate: 39% 22.4% ELL 13.07% Sp. Ed.	Arizona's Instrument of Measured Standards Stanford 9 NWEA	
Florida Community College Jacksonville, FL	90,000			Accuplacer College Placement Test on Writing, Reading, and Math	
Georgia Perimeter College Clarkston, GA	21,000	Average age: 24.9 Median age: 22 Full time: 45.5% Non-U.S. citizens: 2,895 Male: 37.7% Female: 62.3%		COMPASS Writing Exam Regent's Essay Exam (state mandated)	HOPE Scholarship (funded by GA lotteries) scholarships, grants, loans, work studies
Greenville Technical College Greenville, SC	17,079	Female: 7,121 (59%) Male: 4,922 (41%) 73.3% White 21.1% Black 2.6% Hispanic 1.7% Asian/Pacific Islander		ASSET	Bedford-St. Martin's and Prentice Hall; Greenville Schools District; The Open Book; GTC Office of Academic Support; Office of Planning and Grants; Arts and Sciences Div.; English Dept.
John Tyler Community College Chester, VA	6,092; 1,641 full- and 4,451 part-time	Female: 64.31% Male: 35% 67.39% White 25.16% Black 2.64% Asian 2.42% Other 2.36% Hispanic 56.18% Ages 17–24 43.82% Ages 25 older	35% of students admitted qualify for Pell Grants	COMPASS and SAT for writing placement	

Institution	Pop.	Demographics	Socioeconomic	Writing Assessment Tool	Aux. Funding
J. Sargeant Reynolds Community College Richmond, VA	5,600	Female: 62% Male: 38% 72% White 22% Black 6% Other	46% on financial aid	COMPASS Placement Test at admission; no exit test	
Lee-Davis High School Hanover County, VA	1,534	Female: 52% Male: 48% 87% White 8% Black 5% Other		State-mandated Writing SOL test in grade 10 and Reading and Literature SOL test in grade 11	
Lloyd C. Bird High School Chester, VA	1,845	72.5% White 23.5% Black 5% Black and Asian	28% qualify for government aid	State-mandated Writing SOL test in grade 10 and Reading and Literature SOL test in grade 11	2004, Chesterfield Co.—SOL funding for high school writing center staff
Ross Beatty High School Cassopolis, MI	514	Male: 244 Female: 270 White: 329 Black: 157 Asian: 18 Hispanic: 10	free lunch: 171 reduced-price lunch: 40	M.E.A.P Michigan Educational Assessment Program	
Samuel W. Wolfson Senior High School Jacksonville, FL	1,990	53% Black 38% White 9% Immigrant ESL	free or reduced lunch: 43%	FCAT at grade 10 Florida Writes at grade 10	
Southwestern Michigan College Dowagiac, MI	2,948	White: 77.8% Black: 6.5% Hispanic: 4.3% Asian: 0.9% Native American: 1.2%	1198 Pell Awards	ACT SAT PSAT MEAP Writing	

Institution	Pop.	Demographics	Socioeconomic	Writing Assessment Tool	Aux. Funding
Tidewater Community College/Norfolk Virginia Beach, VA	35,000	Female: 59.46% Male: 40.54% 57.30% White 30.89% Black 11.81% Other		COMPASS Reading, Writing, and Mathematics Placement; test at admission	
Virginia Beach City Public Schools Virginia Beach, VA	74,682	White: 44,218 Black: 21,051 Hispanic: 3,566 Native American: 251 Asian/Pacific Islander: 4,422 Unspecified: 1,174	free or reduced lunch: 21,790 (28.3%)	Standards of Learning (SOL) Reading and Writing	
Woodmont High School Piedmont, SC	1,000			South Carolina Exit Exam	

Editor

With over three decades of experience in instruction and supervision in secondary and postsecondary education, **Chris Jennings Dixon** has established exemplary credentials in writing curriculum, developed innovative language arts programs, and organized novel approaches to instruction.

After earning her BS in English education from Longwood College, Farmville, Virginia, and masters in English from Virginia Commonwealth University, Richmond, Virginia, Chris completed postgraduate work at the University of Virginia, Charlottesville, and Appalachian State University, Boone, North Carolina. She taught English, composition, and journalism in high schools and colleges for thirty-eight years in Henrico County, Richmond, and Virginia Beach, Virginia. From 1998–2005, as associate professor of English at the Virginia Beach Campus of Tidewater Community College, she designed and directed two U.S. Department of Education Fund for the Improvement of Secondary Education grant projects to align writing instruction and improve high school students' preparation for college writing. For her work in facilitating writing partnerships among secondary and postsecondary institutions across the state and nation, Chris received the 2004 Leon F. Williams Award for Significant Contribution to English Language Arts from the Virginia Association of Teachers and the 2003 Outstanding Program in English from the Conference on College Composition and Communication's Two-Year College English Association.

Following her retirement on June 1, 2005, Tidewater Community College conferred the honor of professor emeritus on Chris for meritorious and significant service to the college. As a promoter of portfolio methodology for assessment of writing; trainer of students and teachers in writing center strategies; facilitator of collaborative workshops for teachers in middle school, high school, and college and university settings across the state and nation; NCTE consultant on teaching writing; and author/editor of *Lesson Plans for Teaching Writing*, Chris continues to make significant contributions to the field of English education.

Contributors

Mary Virginia Allen teaches developmental English and first-year composition at Greenville Technical College. She is a former English teacher at Woodmont High School in Greenville, South Carolina. She has seven years of teaching experience.

Susan P. Allen is professor and associate department head at Greenville Technical College, Greenville, South Carolina, teaching developmental English, first-year composition, and sophomore literature. She has won numerous awards for excellence in teaching and has twenty-six years of teaching experience.

Elizabeth H. Beagle teaches English at Landstown High School, Virginia Beach, Virginia. She has fourteen years of teaching experience.

James Blasingame Jr. is assistant professor of English at Arizona State University, Tempe. His graduate studies focused on teaching adolescent literature.

Suzy S. Bolton teaches both regular and AP English at Lloyd C. Bird High School, Chesterfield County, Virginia. She is also a sponsor of the student newspaper, assistant to the Chesterfield County instructional specialist, and joint instructor of SOL remediation. She has twenty-six years of teaching experience.

Sherri Bova teaches regular and honors English at Lloyd C. Bird High School, Chesterfield County, Virginia. She was 2004 Teacher of the Year, sponsors the senior class, and has eighteen years of teaching experience.

Marty Brooks is associate professor of English at John Tyler Community College, Chester, Virginia, teaching first-year composition, American literature, 200-level composition, and developmental composition. She has published numerous articles in anthologies and periodicals and has nine years of teaching experience.

Reginald Bruster is associate professor of English at Greenville Technical College, Greenville, South Carolina, teaching composition as well as American, British, and world literatures. He has twice been honored as Greenville Technical College Arts and Sciences Division Faculty of the Year, and he has fifteen years of teaching experience.

Sue Buck teaches English and is department chair at Ross Beatty High School, Cassopolis, Michigan.

Ramona Clark teaches English at Green Run High School, Virginia Beach, Virginia. She is a Tidewater Writing Fellow, received the Virginia Association of Teachers of English Service Award, and has twenty-nine years of teaching experience.

Mary Kay Crouch is associate professor of English at California State University, Fullerton, specializing in composition, language, and literacy. She has published an article, reviews, and a book chapter; won CSU, Fullerton's Collaborative Teaching Award; and has thirty-five years of teaching experience.

Dale DeSarro teaches English and is department co-chair at Green Run High School, Virginia Beach, Virginia.

Dorothy K. Fletcher teaches English and creative writing at Wolfson High School, Jacksonville, Florida. She has published both fiction and poetry and has thirty years of teaching experience.

Jennifer Fletcher teaches regular, honors, and AP English and is department chair at Buena Park High School, Buena Park, California. She is also adjunct faculty at Concordia University, Irvine. Fletcher received a PhD from the University of California, Irvine, and has ten years of teaching experience.

Thomas J. Hargrove is instructor of English at Tidewater Community College, Virginia Beach, Virginia, specializing in developmental and English composition.

Susan S. Hawkes is a former teacher of writing and literature at Lloyd C. Bird High School, Chesterfield County, Virginia. She is also a creative writer and has thirty-one years of teaching experience.

Julie Herwick teaches English at Ross Beatty High School, Cassopolis, Michigan.

Charles W. Hoofnagle is adjunct instructor of reading and writing at Tidewater Community College, Portsmouth, Virginia. He has received TCC Faculty Recognition for fifteen years and has more than thirty-eight years of teaching experience.

Michelle Huff is a former teacher of grades 9–12 English at Samuel Wolfson High School, Jacksonville, Florida.

Ann Louise Johnston is professor of English at Tidewater Community College, Virginia Beach, Virginia; courses include Intermediate Advanced Bridge to College English, developmental literature, linguistics, and ESL teaching methods. She is a former high school teacher and has published numerous articles. Johnston has forty years of teaching experience.

Wendy C. Kelleher is the site supervisor for service learning/English at Arizona State University and teaches composition and methods of teaching composition. She has published several articles, received numerous fellowships, and has twelve years of teaching experience.

Joseph H. Lemrow is instructor of English at Southwestern Michigan College in Dowagiac. He has published articles and book reviews and presented on composition and literature at various conferences; he has forty years of teaching experience.

Michele Marits is an instructor at Tidewater Community College, Virginia Beach, Virginia, focusing on developmental and English composition. She has nine years of teaching experience.

Miles McCrimmon is professor of English at J. Sargeant Reynolds Community College, Richmond, Virginia. He has twenty years of teaching experience.

David Meyerholz teaches government at Salem High School, Virginia Beach, Virginia.

Stuart D. Noel is assistant professor of English at Georgia Perimeter College in Clarkston. He has nine years of teaching experience.

Charles S. Pierce Jr. is professor of English at Tidewater Community College, Virginia Beach, Virginia, focusing on developmental and English composition.

Melissa Reid teaches language arts at Fees Middle School, Tempe, Arizona.

Melissa Revel teaches grade 7 language arts at Fees Middle School, Tempe, Arizona. She has two years of teaching experience.

Mary F. Rezac teaches social studies and grade 6 language arts at Fees Middle School, Tempe, Arizona. She has thirty years of teaching experience.

Frances G. Sharer is a high school English instructional specialist for the Virginia Beach City Public Schools, as well as curriculum consultant/writer for grades 9–12. She has published in several publications and has twenty-seven years of teaching experience.

Susan B. Slavicz is professor of English at Florida Community College, Jacksonville. She has twenty-five years of teaching experience.

Christopher Smutzer is an instructional specialist and former teacher at Woodmont High School, Greenville, South Carolina. He was 2000–2001 Woodmont High School Teacher of the Year and has fourteen years of teaching experience.

Bonnie Startt is an instructor at Tidewater Community College, Virginia Beach, Virginia, focusing on developmental and English composition. She has fifteen years of teaching experience.

Regina D. Taylor teaches grades 9–12 English at Buena Park High School, Buena Park, California.

Shanita Williams formerly taught English at Kellam High School, Virginia Beach, Virginia. She has nine years of teaching experience.

This book was typeset in Palatino and Helvetica by Electronic Imaging.
The typeface used on the cover was Interstate.
The book was printed on 50-lb. Williamsburg Offset paper by Versa Press, Inc.